Quer durchs Tiergartenviertel

Das historische Quartier und seine Bewohner

Through the Tiergartenviertel

The Historic District and Its Residents

Quer durchs   Katrin Wehry
Tiergartenviertel
Das historische Quartier und seine Bewohner

Für die Staatlichen Museen zu Berlin herausgegeben von Michael Eissenhauer

MICHAEL IMHOF VERLAG

Luftaufnahme auf das Kulturforum an der Potsdamer Straße in Tiergarten, 1978.

Aerial view onto the Kulturforum on Potsdamer Straße, Tiergarten district, 1978.

Vorwort

Das Berliner Kulturforum versammelt heute einzigartige Institutionen von Weltrang. Hier befinden sich die Philharmonie, die Staatsbibliothek, das Musikinstrumenten-Museum und der Kammermusiksaal nach Entwürfen Hans Scharouns, die zum Teil erst nach seinem Tod realisiert wurden. Ebenso wichtig sind die Neue Nationalgalerie von Ludwig Mies van der Rohe, das Kunstgewerbemuseum, die Kunstbibliothek und das Kupferstichkabinett nach den Planungen des Architekten Rolf Gutbrod sowie die Gemäldegalerie von Heinz Hilmer und Christoph Sattler. Die Benennung „Kulturforum" verspricht dem Besucher ein zusammenhängendes Ensemble, jedoch zeigt sich vor Ort ein anderes Bild: lose gruppierte Gebäude, in deren Mitte neben der Potsdamer Straße die Freifläche vor der historischen St. Matthäus-Kirche von Friedrich August Stüler, die das Areal weit mehr trennen als vereinen. Bis in die Gegenwart ist dem Ort seine wechselvolle Geschichte und die ehemalige Randlage anzumerken; auch 70 Jahre nach dem Ende des Zweiten Weltkriegs und mehr als 25 Jahre nach dem Mauerfall ist es noch nicht gelungen, das Kulturforum in einen angemessenen städtebaulichen Kontext zu stellen.

Flächendeckende Bombardierungen während des Zweiten Weltkriegs und die zuvor von den Nationalsozialisten durchgeführten Zerstörungen im Rahmen der NS-Planung für die Hauptstadt „Germania" hatten 1945 eine große Brache hinterlassen. Die Neuordnung nach dem Zweiten Weltkrieg ge-

Foreword

Berlin's Kulturforum is today the address of a number of unique cultural institutions of international standing. This is the location of the Philharmonie, the Staatsbibliothek, the Musikinstrumenten-Museum (Museum of Musical Instruments) and the Kammermusiksaal, all designed by Hans Scharoun, who did not live to see all of them completed. Equally significant are the Neue Nationalgalerie (New National Gallery) designed by Ludwig Mies van der Rohe, the Kunstgewerbemuseum (Museum of Decorative Arts), the Kunstbibliothek (Art Library) and the Kupferstichkabinett (Museum of Prints and Drawings) by Rolf Gutbrod and the Gemäldegalerie (Gallery of Old Masters) by Heinz Hilmer and Christoph Sattler. The name "Kulturforum" might conjure up the image of a cohesive ensemble, but visitors are, in fact, greeted by a quite different picture: a loose assemblage of buildings which is cloven rather than held together by Potsdamer Straße and the open space outside Friedrich August Stüler's Matthäus Church. The location still betrays its eventful history and its years as a backwater on the eastern margin of West Berlin. 70 years after the end of the Second World War and more than 25 years after the fall of the Wall the Kulturforum has not yet acquired the urban architectural setting it deserves.

In 1945 the site was a wasteland, the result of carpet bombing in the Second World War and the demolition of buildings to make way for construction of the National Socialists' capital, "Germania". The task

staltete sich schwierig. Bereits 1946 hatte der Architekt Hans Scharoun, der ein Jahr zuvor zum Stadtrat für Bau- und Wohnungswesen ernannt wurde, erste Ideen für einen Kollektivplan vorgelegt und diese 1957/58 im Rahmen des Hauptstadtwettbewerbs sowie 1964 für die Ausschreibung zum Neubau der Staatsbibliothek konkretisiert. Umgesetzt werden konnten die übergreifenden Raumkonzepte Scharouns nicht, Grund dafür waren verschiedene Faktoren wie eine geänderte Verkehrsplanung. Vielmehr folgten in regelmäßigen Abständen neue Vorschläge, basierend auf den Berlin-Verträgen von 1971/72, die Vorstellung eines Zentralen Bereichs, der in die Stadt- und Verkehrsplanung gedanklich auch den Berliner Ostteil einbezog. Besonders heftige Debatten löste der von dem österreichischen Architekten Hans Hollein eingereichte Beitrag zum Internationalen Gutachterverfahren „Kulturforum" 1983 aus, in dem Hollein unter Hinzufügung eines Turms, von Kolonnaden und eines Kanals Bezüge zwischen den einzelnen Gebäuden herstellen und ihnen Zusammenhalt geben wollte. Auch die nach dem Mauerfall geführten Kontroversen haben kein stimmiges Konzept für die Weiterentwicklung des Kulturforums geliefert. Nach jahrelangen Diskussionen wurde 2005/06 vom Senat und dem Abgeordnetenhaus auf Grundlage der Scharoun'schen Planungen ein Masterplan zur Weiterentwicklung des Kulturforums beschlossen, der jedoch nicht umgesetzt wurde. Allerdings liegt seit Juni 2011 auf seiner Basis eine

of redesigning the area after the War proved a tricky one. As early as 1945 the architect Hans Scharoun, the new city councillor in charge of construction and housing, had set out some preliminary ideas for a collective plan, ideas which he enlarged on in 1957/58 when responding to the call for bids in a competition to redesign the former capital, Berlin, and in 1964 when submitting a design for the reconstruction of the Staatsbibliothek. Due to a number of factors that included changes in transportation planning Scharoun's vision could not be realised. Instead there was a steady flow of proposals based on the Berlin Agreements of 1971/72 and also the notion of a *Central Area* straddling the border between the two Berlins. One particularly controversial debate was triggered by the Austrian architect Hans Hollein's submission for the Kulturforum International Assessment in 1983, which envisioned using colonnades, a tower and a canal to establish a cohesive spatial relation between the various buildings. Yet post-Wall controversies, too, have been no more successful in presenting a coherent plan for the development of the Kulturforum. After years of discussions the Senate and Berlin Parliament agreed on a master plan based on Scharoun's designs, which again was not realised. This notwithstanding, in June 2011 an initial plan for the gradual implementation of Scharoun's "open space" project was submitted and the first phases of this plan have been executed. In 2012 the location was again in the public eye thanks

Vorplanung zur schrittweisen Realisierung des Freiraumkonzeptes vor, dessen erste Schritte eingeleitet und verwirklicht wurden. Neue Aufmerksamkeit erfuhr der Standort 2012 durch eine weltweit geführte Debatte um den Umzug der Gemäldegalerie auf die Museumsinsel. Daraus resultierend beschloss der Bundestag im November 2014, einen Erweiterungsbau für die Kunst des 20. Jahrhunderts in Angriff zu nehmen und damit die räumlich beengte Sammlung der Nationalgalerie zu entlasten. Eine in dieser Folge erforderliche, umfassende Planung für das gesamte Kulturforum steht weiterhin aus. Als Schritt in diese Richtung haben die Staatlichen Museen zu Berlin 2015 ein internes Positionspapier für ihren Bedarf erarbeitet, das die erforderlichen Leitlinien der zukünftigen Entwicklung des Kulturforums – dieses neben der Museumsinsel wichtigsten Standorts der Staatlichen Museen zu Berlin – formuliert.

Heute fällt es schwer zu glauben, dass sich um das Jahr 1900 genau in dieser Gegend eines der attraktivsten Wohngebiete Berlins befand, das Tiergartenviertel, welches sich zwischen der Tiergartenstraße im Norden, der Bendlerstraße (seit 1955 Stauffenbergstraße), dem Landwehrkanal im Süden und der Potsdamer Straße erstreckte. Hier hielt die Moderne Einzug in Berlin, hier wurden die ersten französischen Impressionisten präsentiert, hier ließen sich innovative Künstler und Galeristen, Sammler und Mäzene nieder, hier entstanden eine Vielzahl an Bauten namhafter Architekten. Neben reichen Industriellen in

to an international debate on the Gemäldegalerie's move to the Museumsinsel (Museum Island). In November 2014, as a result of this heart-searching, the Bundestag resolved to commission the construction of an extension to house 20th-century artworks and, in so doing, to reduce the pressure on the Nationalgalerie's collection, which is too large for its current premises. There is still no comprehensive planning concept for the Kulturforum as a whole, a plan of action rendered essential by this extension to the Gemäldegalerie. In 2015 the Staatliche Museen zu Berlin (National Museums in Berlin) took a step in this direction by drawing up an internal policy document for its own use. The document sets out the requisite guidelines for the future development of the Kulturforum, the second most important site of the Staatliche Museen zu Berlin after the Museumsinsel.

Today it is hard to believe that circa 1900 this area was one of the finest residential locations in Berlin. This was the Tiergarten district, covering an area bounded by Tiergartenstraße to the north, Bendlerstraße (renamed Stauffenbergstraße in 1955), the Landwehrkanal to the south and Potsdamer Straße. This part of Berlin was where modernity was making itself felt, where the first French Impressionists were being shown, where innovative artists, gallery owners, collectors and art patrons were setting up house and where high-profile architects were hard at work. Wealthy industrialists in handsome villas rubbed shoulders here with artists and other creat-

prächtigen Villen lebten an diesem Ort Kulturschaffende in Mietwohnungen, ein Austausch zwischen den Gruppen fand in den Kultureinrichtungen und Salons sowie den Cafés und Gaststätten statt. Zeugnis von dieser Zeit geben nur noch wenige Gebäude: die St. Matthäus-Kirche in der Mitte des heutigen Kulturforums, die in die Gemäldegalerie integrierte Villa Parey und die Villa Gontard, der Sitz der Generaldirektion der Staatlichen Museen zu Berlin, in der Stauffenbergstraße. Einen Eindruck dieses vielseitigen Viertels können uns zeitgenössische Fotografien geben, von denen sich eine Vielzahl auch prominenter Fotografen wie Waldemar Titzenthaler erhalten haben, und mit deren Hilfe Ihnen im Folgenden ausgewählte Orte und Bewohner des Tiergartenviertels vorgestellt werden.

Michael Eissenhauer
Generaldirektor der Staatlichen Museen zu Berlin

ive types renting rooms in tenement blocks. People from many different walks of life jostled and consorted with each other at cultural venues and in salons, cafés and restaurants. Few buildings from that era survive today. Examples are the Matthäus Church, located at the centre of today's Kulturforum, the Villa Parey, which forms part of the Gemäldegalerie, and the Villa Gontard on Stauffenbergstraße, which houses the offices of the General Directorate of the Staatliche Museen zu Berlin. The diversity of this district is revealed in photographs from that period, many of which were the work of big-name photographers such as Waldemar Titzenthaler. Their pictures are an important contribution to this showcase of selected locations and residents of the Tiergarten district.

Michael Eissenhauer
Director General of the Staatliche Museen zu Berlin

Einführung

Introduction

Das Berliner Tiergartenviertel entwickelte sich seit dem Ende des 18. Jahrhunderts von einem öffentlichen Lustpark zunächst zu einem Ort für die Sommerfrische vor den Toren der Stadt und ab Mitte des 19. Jahrhunderts zu einem bevorzugten Wohngebiet vor allem für Angehörige des Berliner Bürgertums. Räumliche Veränderungen wie die Gestaltung eines Landschaftsgartens im Tiergarten durch Peter Joseph Lenné (1789−1866) bis 1840, die Anlage des Landwehrkanals mit begrünten Alleen auf beiden Uferseiten bis 1850 und die immer dichter werdende Bebauung des Zentrums erhöhten die Attraktivität des Viertels, welches bis zur Mitte des 19. Jahrhunderts nicht zum innerstädtischen Bereich zählte.

Den Bewohnern bot das Viertel Platz für verschiedene Lebensweisen: Rund um die St. Matthäus-Kirche entstanden um die Jahrhundertwende vorrangig mehrgeschossige Wohnhäuser sowie Stadt- und Mietvillen, entlang der Tiergartenstraße befanden sich dagegen weiterhin frei stehende Villen mit weitläufigen Gartenanlagen. Neben sehr reichen Industriellen fanden hier auch Künstler mit geringerem Einkommen eine Wohnung. Vertreter verschiedener sozialer Schichten trafen sich unter anderem in den zahlreichen Salons, die in erster Linie von Frauen initiiert wurden und zumeist politisch oder kulturell ausgerichtet waren. Die Anziehung der Viertels ergab sich auch durch die in unmittelbarer Nähe liegenden pulsierenden, großstädtischen Areale: Der Potsdamer Platz, der verkehrsreichste Ort des Deut-

From the end of the 18th century onwards Berlin's Tiergarten district (Tiergartenviertel) grew from a recreational park into a destination for city dwellers seeking summer respite from the city and from the mid 19th century into the residential address of choice for Berlin's middle classes. Developments such as the creation by Peter Joseph Lenné (1789−1866) of a landscaped park in the Tiergarten, completed in 1840, the formalisation of the Landwehrkanal with tree-lined avenues on each bank, completed in 1850, and the ongoing construction of new buildings in the district all raised the cachet of the area, which until the mid 19th century did not form part of Berlin's inner city.

The neighbourhood offered its residents a range of housing options and lifestyles. The turn of the century saw multi-storey residential blocks and modest villas designed for tenant occupancy spring up around the Matthäus Church, while the Tiergartenstraße attracted detached villas with extensive gardens. Impecunious artists and rich industrialists alike could find suitable rental accommodation here. People from all walks of life met in one or other of the many salons, most of which were initiated by women and were politically or culturally oriented. The throbbing centres of big-city activity nearby were another draw for prospective residents. Chief among these were Potsdamer Platz, the busiest traffic hub in Germany, site of the first underground rail departure (1902), the first German radio broad-

schen Reiches, von dem aus 1902 die erste U-Bahn Berlins fuhr, 1923 die erste deutsche Radiosendung übertragen wurde oder 1924 die erste Verkehrsampel Berlins stand, und der Leipziger Platz mit dem prächtigen Warenhaus Wertheim. Eine große Auswahl an Cafés und Gaststätten, Hotels und Vergnügungslokalen sowie Galerien und Kunsthandlungen waren schnell erreichbar.

Im Tiergartenviertel lebten viele prominente Persönlichkeiten mit ständigem Wohnsitz, zu ihnen gehörten Künstler wie der Bildhauer und Maler Georg Kolbe (1877−1947) und die Maler Adolph von Menzel (1815−1905) und Anton von Werner (1843−1915). Außerdem eröffneten in der Gegend eine Reihe von Galerien und Kunsthandlungen, darunter die der Cousins Bruno Cassirer (1872−1941) und Paul Cassirer (1871−1926), die zunächst gemeinsam und später getrennt als Verleger, Galeristen und Kunsthändler tätig waren. Gleichzeitig ließen sich hier Wissenschaftler wie der Archäologe Ernst Curtius (1814−98), Schriftsteller wie Julius Elias (1861−1925) und Carl Zuckmayer (1896–1977) oder wohlhabende Unternehmer und Kunstmäzene wie Eduard Arnhold (1849−1925) nieder. Von den im Tiergartenviertel lebenden Frauen sind einige noch heute durch ihre gesellschaftlichen Salons bekannt, so Marie von Olfers (1826−1924) oder Cornelie Richter (1842−1922).

Neben den berühmten und weniger bekannten Anwohnern befanden sich im Viertel aber auch öffent-

cast (1923) and the first set of traffic lights in the city (1924), and Leipziger Platz, with its magnificent Wertheim department store. Residents were a short walk or ride away from galleries, art dealerships, hotels, cafés, restaurants and assorted establishments geared to amusement and recreation.

The Tiergarten district was home to many celebrities. Artists living long-term here included the sculptor and painter Georg Kolbe (1877−1947) and the painters Adolph von Menzel (1815−1905) and Anton von Werner (1843−1915). A number of galleries and art dealerships opened in the area, among them those of the cousins Bruno Cassirer (1872−1941) and Paul Cassirer (1871−1926), who worked first together and afterwards separately as publishers, gallery owners and art dealers. Settlers to the area included scientists such was Ernst Curtius (1814−98), writers like Julius Elias (1861−1925) and Carl Zuckmayer (1896–1977) and wealthy entrepreneurs and art patrons like Eduard Arnhold (1849−1925). And the names of some women – Marie von Olfers (1826−1924) and Cornelie Richter (1842−1922) and others − still feature in the local lore for their salons frequented by all and sundry.

Aside from the prominent and not-so-famous individuals that took up residence, the area also attracted public institutions such as embassies, a trend that began in 1888 with the arrival of the Chinese embassy and culminated in the 1930s, when the district

liche Institutionen wie die Botschaften zahlreicher Länder; eine Entwicklung, die 1888 mit der Chinesischen Botschaft ihren Anfang nahm und die in den 1930er-Jahren in einer Anzahl von über 30 Botschaften und annähernd so vielen Konsulaten gipfelte. Die Diplomaten der Botschaften fanden ihre Wohnungen in direkter Nachbarschaft. Außerdem gab es große Verwaltungsgebäude, zum Beispiel das Landratsamt des Kreises Teltow, welches ab 1889/90 in der Victoriastraße 17 und 18 unter anderem für den erst seit 1920 zu Berlin gehörenden Bezirk Schöneberg zuständig war, oder die Teltower Kriegswirtschafts-Gesellschaft ab 1917/18 in der Matthäikirchstraße 10.

Von der beeindruckenden Geschichte und der repräsentativen Gestalt des ehemaligen Tiergartenviertels zeigt sich dem heutigen Besucher nur noch ein kleiner Bruchteil in Form der ganz wenigen erhaltenen und wiederaufgebauten Gebäude: die St. Matthäus-Kirche in der Mitte des Areals, die Villa Gontard in der Stauffenbergstraße – heute Sitz der Generaldirektion der Staatlichen Museen zu Berlin – und die in die Gemäldegalerie integrierte Villa Parey. Einen Einblick in das ehemals äußerst lebhafte Quartier können heute noch alte Fotografien geben, deshalb sollen im Folgenden rund 40 der einstigen angesehenen Bewohner des Tiergartenviertels mit je einer Porträtfotografie und einer Aufnahme ihres Wohnumfeldes vorgestellt werden. Ergänzend sind Abbildungen einiger markanter städtebaulicher Plätze und Straßenzüge des historischen Viertel ein-

counted over thirty embassies and almost as many consulates. Embassy diplomats lived in the immediate vicinity of their workplaces. There were also large administrative buildings such as the offices of Teltow District, located at Victoriastraße 17 and 18 from 1889/90 onwards and responsible for the borough of Schöneberg, which was incorporated into Berlin only in 1920, and the Teltow War-Economy Society, which set up offices at Matthäikirchstraße 10.

Today's visitor will find only a few surviving allusions to the impressive history and prestigious face of the former Tiergarten district. These remnants of a bygone age come in the form of a very few buildings that have withstood the ravages of time or been restored to their former glory – the Matthäus Church at the centre of the district, the Villa Gontard on Stauffenbergstraße – today the offices of the Staatliche Museen zu Berlin – and the Villa Parey, today part of the Gemäldegalerie (Gallery of Old Masters). Old photographs from that period afford a glimpse into a neighbourhood teeming with life, which is why the following presentation of fifty or so of the district's highly esteemed inhabitants will include a portrait photo of each of them and a picture of their immediate environment. There will also be photos of selected streets and squares throughout the historic quarter, whose original buildings and street features have all but vanished. In some cases modern-day photos of the same locations are juxtaposed with the old.

gefügt, von deren Substanz heute so gut wie nichts mehr erhalten ist, in einzelnen Fällen sind ihnen aktuelle Fotografien zur Seite gestellt.

Doch betrachten wir zunächst das Areal des alten Tiergartenviertels mithilfe eines historischen Rundgangs durch die einzelnen Straßenzüge; zur Orientierung befindet sich im vorderen Einband des Buches ein Kartenausschnitt von 1910, im hinteren ein aktueller Plan. In der Mitte des Viertels steht die 1844 bis 1846 errichtete, dem Apostel und Evangelisten Matthäus geweihte St. Matthäus-Kirche, die im Zweiten Weltkrieg schwer beschädigt worden war und bis 1960 wiederaufgebaut wurde. Vor dem Krieg erschloss die Matthäikirchstraße nördlich und südlich die Kirche, heute steht auf dem ehemals südlichen Straßenabschnitt die Neue Nationalgalerie, der noch existierende nördliche Teil wurde hier, nahe der Philharmonie, 1998 nach dem langjährigen Chefdirigenten des Berliner Philharmonischen Orchesters Herbert von Karajan (1908−89) benannt.

In unmittelbarer Nachbarschaft um die St. Matthäus-Kirche befanden sich vor dem Zweiten Weltkrieg gleich drei Straßen, die Namen von Mitgliedern aus der Familie des sogenannten 99-Tage-Kaisers, Friedrich III. (1831−88), trugen. So begann westlich der Kirche die Sigismundstraße, die im Jahr 1865 nach dem kurz zuvor geborenen und wenig später verstorbenen Sohn Friedrichs III. benannt wurde. Die Sigismundstraße, in der sich heute mit der ehemaligen Villa Parey eines der seltenen erhaltenen Ge-

First, however, let us explore the area by taking a tour through the streets and looking at the history of the area. There are maps to serve as a guide, one dating from 1910 inside the front cover and a modern-day plan of the area inside the back cover. In the centre of the district stands the Matthäus Church, dedicated to the Apostle Matthew. Built between 1844 and 1846, it suffered serious damage in the Second World War and reconstruction was completed in 1960. Before the war Matthäikirchstraße ran north and south of the church. The street's former southern section is today the site of the Neue Nationalgalerie (New National Gallery) and in 1998 the northern portion was renamed in honour of Herbert von Karajan (1908−89) after the principal conductor of the nearby Berliner Philharmonie.

Prior to the war and in the immediate vicinity of the Matthäus Church three streets bore the names of family members of the "99-day emperor", Friedrich III (1831−88). Sigismundstraße, which began to the west of the church, was named in 1865 after Friedrich's son, who was born shortly before and died soon afterwards. Sigismundstraße, which features one of the Tiergartenviertel's few surviving houses – now incorporated into the Gemäldegalerie – is also one of the few streets in the immediate area that has retained its original name. Almost all streets were renamed during the Nazi period. Today the street between Potsdamer and Stauffenberg streets is considerably longer than it was in the interwar period,

bäude befindet – integriert in die Gemäldegalerie – ist außerdem eine der wenigen Straßen in der direkten Umgebung, die durchgehend seit 1865 ihren Namen behielt; fast alle Straßen waren zumindest in der NS-Zeit umbenannt. Ihr Verlauf ist heute zwischen Stauffenbergstraße und Potsdamer Straße wesentlich länger als vor dem Zweiten Weltkrieg, reichte sie doch ursprünglich nur bis zur nächsten Querstraße. Ebenfalls auf ein Mitglied der Königlichen Familie verweisend, nämlich auf die jüngste Tochter Friedrichs III., verlief auf der anderen Seite der St. Matthäus-Kirche die Margaretenstraße (bis 1902 Margarethenstraße). Die Straße führte ursprünglich von der Matthäikirchstraße bis zur alten Potsdamer Straße, nach dem Zweiten Weltkrieg wurde sie auf rund die Hälfte ihrer ursprünglichen Länge verkürzt und als Bauland ausgewiesen, seit 1993 heißt der verbliebene Teil Scharounstraße, nach dem Architekten der benachbarten Philharmonie und Staatsbibliothek Hans Scharoun (1893–72). Bereits seit ihrem Hochzeitsjahr 1858 trug die sie kreuzende Straße den Namen Victorias (1840–1901), der Frau Friedrichs III. und Tochter der englischen Queen Victoria. Die Straße verlief von der Tiergartenstraße bis zur Königin-Augusta-Straße, sie existierte bis 1970 und ging dann in der heutigen Potsdamer Straße auf.

Über die alte Potsdamer Straße, die ursprünglich linear von der Potsdamer Brücke zum Potsdamer Platz verlief, dann aber nach dem Zweiten Weltkrieg in einem nordwestlichen Bogen um das Gelände der

when it extended only one block. On the other side of the church was another street with royal connections, Margaretenstraße (spelt Margarethenstraße until 1902), named after Friedrich III's youngest daughter. Running originally from Matthäikirchstraße to the former route of Potsdamer Straße, the street was shortened after the war to half its original length and re-zoned as building land. In 1993 the remaining western half changed its name to Scharounstraße in honour of the architect of the neighbouring Philharmonie and Staatsbibliothek, Hans Scharoun (1893–72). This street was intersected by Victoriastraße, christened thus to mark the wedding in 1858 of Victoria (1840–1901), the wife of Friedrich III and daughter of the English Queen Victoria. The street ran from Tiergartenstraße to Königin-Augusta-Straße and was merged into today's Potsdamer Straße in 1970.

Moving along the old Potsdamer Straße, which used to follow a straight line from the Potsdamer Bridge to Potsdamer Platz but now traces a right-hand curve around the Staatsbibliothek, erected in 1978, we now continue our tour through Potsdamer Platz into Königgrätzer Straße. The name of this street recalls Prussia's decisive 1866 victory against Austria near Königgrätz. Today the street is split into Ebertstraße and Stresemannstraße. Turning left into Lennéstraße, named after Peter Joseph Lenné, landscape architect and designer of the adjacent Tiergarten, we arrive at Kemperplatz, whose name com-

Ostansicht der St. Matthäus-Kirche, 2015.

East view of Matthäus Church, 2015.

Die St. Matthäus-Kirche wurde 1844–46 von dem Architekten August Stüler (1800–65) auf Initiative wohlhabender Bürger errichtet, das Patronat übernahm Friedrich Wilhelm IV. Der Wiederaufbau nach Zerstörungen im Zweiten Weltkrieg erfolgte 1956–61 durch Paul und Jürgen Emmerich. Abbildung um 1920.

The Matthäus Church was built in 1844–46 by the architect August Stüler (1800–65). Construction was initiated by a group of wealthy citizens, with Friedrich Wilhelm IV as patron. Reconstruction after the Second World War was undertaken by Paul and Jürgen Emmerich in 1956–61. Photograph ca. 1920.

1978 eröffneten Staatsbibliothek gezogen wurde, setzen wir unseren Rundgang entlang des Potsdamer Platzes in die Königgrätzer Straße fort. Der Name dieser Straße gedachte an die 1866 bei Königgrätz ausgetragene, entscheidende Schlacht im Krieg Österreichs gegen Preußen, aus der die preußische Armee siegreich hervorging; heute ist die ehemalige Königgrätzer Straße in die Ebert- und Stresemannstraße unterteilt. Entlang der Lennéstraße, die an den Landschaftsarchitekten und Gestalter des angrenzenden Tiergartens Peter Joseph Lenné erinnert, erreichen wir den Kemperplatz, benannt nach Johann Wilhelm Kemper (1766−1840), der zwischen 1812 und 1830 in unmittelbarer Nähe die viel frequentierte Gaststätte *Kempers Hof* betrieb. Am Kemperplatz befindet sich heute die Einfahrt zum Tiergartentunnel, als Platz ist er kaum noch wahrnehmbar und erst recht findet sich hier kein Hinweis auf die ehemals so prächtige Platzanlage mit dem hoch aufragenden Brunnen in ihrer Mitte.

Vom Kemperplatz blicken wir zunächst in die auf das nahegelegene Schloss verweisende Bellevuestraße, in der sich eines der berühmtesten Hotels in Berlin befand, das Hotel Esplanade. Am Kemperplatz beginnend erschloss sich Richtung Norden in den Tiergarten hinein auch die viel diskutierte, 1901 von Wilhelm II. eingeweihte Siegesallee mit ihren mehr als 30 überlebensgroßen Marmorstatuen der brandenburgischen und preußischen Herrscher. Als prominentes Denkmal sollte sie die Kontinuität des

memorates Johann Wilhelm Kemper (1766−1840), landlord between 1812 and 1830 of the popular restaurant *Kempers Hof*. Today Kemperplatz marks the southern entrance of the Tiergarten tunnel. It is hardly recognisable as a square and there is nothing to suggest that this was once a magnificent space with a fountain spurting at its centre.

From Kemperplatz we look down Bellevuestraße, whose name alludes to the nearby Bellevue Palace. Bellevuestraße is host to the Hotel Esplanade, one of the best-known hotels in Berlin. Kemperplatz also marked the start of the much talked-about Siegesallee, the showpiece boulevard inaugurated in 1901 by Wilhelm II and lined with more than 30 larger-than-life-sized marble statues depicting various rulers of Brandenburg and Prussia. Intended as a symbol of the continuity of the ruling dynasty, this monumental thoroughfare could also be construed as a conservative statement by the Emperor against any avant-garde tendencies in contemporary art.

Returning to Kemperplatz, we now follow Tiergartenstraße until we arrive at two parallel side streets, Regentenstraße and Bendlerstraße. The first received its name in 1860, when the Prussian Prince Wilhelm I was ruling as Prince Regent in the place of his sick brother, Friedrich Wilhelm IV. Since 1947 the street has been called Hitzigallee after Friedrich Hitzig (1811−81), designer of many of the villas in the area. Slightly further west was Bendlerstraße, named after its creator and owner of the adja-

Herrscherhauses betonen, war aber gleichzeitig als konservatives Statement des Kaisers gegen jegliche avantgardistische Ausrichtung der zeitgenössischen Kunst zu verstehen.

Wieder zurück am Kemperplatz verfolgen wir die sich anschließende, am Park entlangführende Tiergartenstraße bis zu zwei parallel verlaufenden Querstraßen: der Regenten- und Bendlerstraße. Die Regentenstraße erhielt ihren Namen 1860 und damit in der Zeit, als der preußische Prinz Wilhelm I. als Prinzregent regierte, also in Vertretung seines erkrankten Bruders Friedrich Wilhelm IV. Seit 1947 heißt sie Hitzigallee nach Friedrich Hitzig (1811–81), dem Architekten zahlreicher Villen im Viertel. Westlich davon erstreckte sich die 1837 nach dem Erschließer und Grundeigentümer der Straße, dem Maurermeister Johann Christoph Bendler (1789–1873), benannte Bendlerstraße, seit 1955 Stauffenbergstraße, in der sich heute in der noch erhaltenen ehemaligen Villa Gontard die Generaldirektion der Staatlichen Museen zu Berlin befindet. Mit den beiden Ufern des Landwehrkanals, der südlichen Grenze des Viertels, beenden wir unseren historischen Rundgang: Die nördliche Uferstraße hieß ab 1867 Königin-Augusta-Straße nach der damaligen preußischen Königin, ihr heutiger Name lautet Reichpietschufer, das südliche Ufer trägt wieder seinen ursprünglichen Namen abgeleitet vom Bezirk Schöneberg.

Das Tiergartenviertel war auch eine Art architektonisches Versuchsfeld, auf dem in einer unglaubli-

cent land, master mason Johann Christoph Bendler (1789–1873). Renamed Stauffenbergstraße in 1955, the street is the location of one of the district's surviving buildings, the former Villa Gontard, which is now home to the Staatliche Museen zu Berlin. We round off our historical tour on the two banks of the Landwehrkanal, which marks the southern fringe of the neighbourhood. From 1867 onwards the street following the northern bank was called Königin-Augusta-Straße after the Prussian queen of the time; it now goes by the name of Reichpietschufer. The south bank has returned to its original nomenclature, denoting the borough of Schöneberg.

The Tiergartenviertel was also a kind of architectural testing ground that spawned an astonishing density of buildings by renowned architects such as Carl Gotthard Langhans (1732–1808), Friedrich Gilly (1772–1800), Ludwig Persius (1803–45), Martin Gropius (1824–80) and Alfred Messel (1853–1909). Prominent among these designers was the aforementioned Friedrich Hitzig, who was barred from public contracts due to his Jewish origins. Up until the 1870s the contracts for public buildings were awarded almost exclusively to Karl Friedrich Schinkel and his successors. So it was that Friedrich August Stüler (1800–65) was commissioned to build the Neues Museum (New Museum) and the Alte Nationalgalerie (Old National Gallery). These public structures usually followed a formula – plaster facades adorned with classicist elements.

chen Dichte Gebäude prominenter Architekten entstanden, so zum Beispiel von Carl Gotthard Langhans (1732–1808), Friedrich Gilly (1772–1800), Ludwig Persius (1803–45), Martin Gropius (1824–80) oder Alfred Messel (1853–1909). Herausgestellt werden kann der bereits genannte Architekt Friedrich Hitzig, dem aufgrund seiner jüdischen Herkunft der Zugang zum Staatsdienst verwehrt blieb. Bis in die 1870er-Jahre erhielten in Berlin fast ausschließlich Karl Friedrich Schinkel und dessen Nachfolger die Aufträge für öffentliche Bauten, so beispielsweise Friedrich August Stüler (1800–65) für das Neue Museum und die Alte Nationalgalerie; sie folgten dabei häufig einem Schema: mit klassizistischen Elementen versehene Fassaden, die zumeist verputzt waren. Friedrich Hitzig dagegen begann hier bei seinen zahlreichen, in den 1850er-Jahren vor allem in der Victoriastraße errichteten Privatvillen zum Beispiel Elemente der römischen Hochrenaissance einzubeziehen. Der Architekt wurde durch diese Bauten so bekannt, dass er renommierte Folgeaufträge aus dem Berliner Bürgertum erhielt, dadurch zu einem der einflussreichsten Privatbaumeister Berlins aufstieg und 1876 sogar zum Präsidenten der Berliner Akademie der Künste ernannt wurde.

Erhalten geblieben ist von dieser unglaublichen architektonischen Fülle des Tiergartenviertels kaum etwas, die 1943 einsetzende Bombardierung hat das Quartier weitgehend zerstört. Doch bereits vor dem Zweiten Weltkrieg hatten die Nationalsozialisten be-

With his many private villas built mostly on Victoriastraße in the 1850s Hitzig began to buck the trend, incorporating elements from the Roman High Renaissance period, a move that raised his profile and led to major commissions from Berlin's middle classes, which in turn made him one of the most influential private architects working in Berlin and led to him being appointed President of Berlin's Academy of Arts in 1876.

Hardly any of this fantastic array of architecture in the Tiergarten district survived the aerial bombings of 1943, which laid waste to the area. Yet even before the war the National Socialists had started expropriating owners – often Jewish – and demolishing buildings to make way for their "North-South Axis" in line with their plans to construct their imperial capital, "Germania". The plans provided for the erection of a "Circular Square", lined with huge buildings, at the point where the "North-South Axis" crossed Potsdamer Straße, on the approximate site of today's Staatsbibliothek. The only building from this project to actually get beyond the drawing board – the House of Tourism – was never completed, surviving as an empty hulk until its demolition in 1962. Mention should also be made of the building at Tiergartenstraße 4, where, in 1940/41, the National Socialists planned "Aktion T4", the murder of over 70,000 physically and mentally disabled people.

In 1957/58, with the architecture competition for the capital, Berlin, attracting bids for building con-

gonnen, für ihre Planungen zur „Reichshauptstadt Germania" zahlreiche Gebäude für die beabsichtigte „Nord-Süd-Achse", häufig von jüdischen Besitzern, zu enteignen und abreißen zu lassen. Gemäß der Planung sollte ungefähr auf dem heutigen Gelände der Staatsbibliothek ein mit monumentalen Gebäuden gesäumter „Runder Platz" als Kreuzungspunkt von „Nord-Süd-Achse" und Potsdamer Straße entstehen. Als einzig tatsächlich begonnenes Projekt wurde das Haus des Fremdenverkehrs jedoch nicht vollendet und blieb bis zu seinem Abriss im Jahr 1962 im Rohbau stehen. Erwähnt werden soll an dieser Stelle außerdem die 1940/41 von den Nationalsozialisten in der Tiergartenstraße 4 geplante, später als „Aktion T4" bezeichnete Ermordung von mehr als 70.000 Menschen mit geistigen und körperlichen Behinderungen.

Nach dem Zweiten Weltkrieg begann mit dem Wettbewerb für die Hauptstadt Berlin 1957/58 die intensive Phase der Neuplanung für das Tiergartenviertel; vorgesehen war nun weiterhin ein Diplomatenviertel im Westen des Areals, im östlichen Teil sollten kulturelle Einrichtungen entstehen. Hans Scharoun (1893–72), der in den folgenden Jahren die neue Philharmonie, die Staatsbibliothek, den Kammermusiksaal und das Institut für Museumsforschung mit dem angegliederten Musikinstrumenten-Museum entwarf – zum Teil nach Scharouns Tod von seinem Partner Edgar Wisniewski (1930–2007) fertiggestellt –, setzte dafür wichtige Impulse. Der städtebauliche Gesamtentwurf von Hans Scharoun

tracts, there began a phase of intensive planning with regard to the Tiergarten district. Plans for the creation of a diplomats' quarter on the western reaches were unchanged and cultural institutions were earmarked for the eastern section. Hans Scharoun was a leading figure in the ensuing building works; in the years that followed he designed the new Philharmonie, the Staatsbibliothek, the Kammermusiksaal and the Institute for Museumsforschung (Institute for Museum Research) with the attached Musikinstrumenten-Museum (Museum of Musical Instruments), some of which were completed by his associate, Edgar Wisniewski (1930–2007), after Scharoun's death. Scharoun's overall design, however, with its notion of a spiritual and cultural link emanating westwards from the Museumsinsel (Museum Island) could not be put into practice. In 1968 the Stiftung Preußischer Kulturbesitz (Prussian Cultural Heritage Foundation) awarded the contract to plan the other new builds at the Kulturforum – the Kunstgewerbemuseum (Museum of Decorative Arts), Kunstbibliothek (Art Library), Kupferstichkabinett (Museum of Prints and Drawings), Gemäldegalerie and Skulpturensammlung (Sculpture Collection) – to the architect Rolf Gutbrod (1910–99). Funding problems and other delays meant that work on the Kunstgewerbemuseum did not start until 1978. At its opening in May 1985 there was such a shower of criticism that the Foundation decided to have Gutbrod finish the sections that he had started – the

mit der Grundidee eines geistigen Bandes der Kultur von der Museumsinsel Richtung Westen, konnte dagegen nicht realisiert werden. Für die Planung der weiteren am Forum beabsichtigten Neubauten, das Kunstgewerbemuseum, die Kunstbibliothek, das Kupferstichkabinett sowie die Gemäldegalerie und die Skulpturensammlung, erhielt 1968 der Architekt Rolf Gutbrod (1910–99) von der Stiftung Preußischer Kulturbesitz den Auftrag. Aufgrund von Verzögerungen durch beispielsweise finanzielle Schwierigkeiten konnte erst 1978 mit dem Kunstgewerbemuseum begonnen werden. Bei dessen Einweihung im Mai 1985 gab es so massive Kritik, dass der Stiftungsrat wenige Monate später beschloss, Rolf Gutbrod die begonnenen Abschnitte beenden zu lassen – die Kunstbibliothek und die in der Mitte gelegene Piazzetta waren im Rohbau fertiggestellt –, aber ansonsten Änderungen vorzunehmen. Im Juni 1986 erfolgte die Ausschreibung für einen Wettbewerb für Gemäldegalerie, den Heinz Hilmer und Christoph Sattler gewannen, die Einweihung der Galerie fand 1998 statt. Der gesamte Komplex rund um die sogenannte Piazzetta zeigt heute deutlich den Antagonismus verschiedener Planungsstufen und die fehlende städtebauliche Einheit mit den Gebäuden Scharouns, der St. Matthäus-Kirche und der Neuen Nationalgalerie Ludwig Mies van der Rohes. Ein verbindliches Gesamtkonzept ist auch nach intensiven, jahrelangen Debatten um die Zukunft des Kulturforums noch nicht gefunden worden.

Kunstbibliothek and the piazzetta at its centre were standing in shell form – but otherwise make changes. June 1986 saw a call for bids to build the Gemäldegalerie, a competition won by Heinz Hilmer and Christoph Sattler; the Gallery opened in 1998. Today the entire complex around the piazzetta points up the antagonism at various stages of planning and reveals the lack of harmony with Scharoun's buildings, the Matthäus Church and the Neue Nationalgalerie of Ludwig Mies van der Rohe. Despite years of intensive debate over the future of the Kulturforum, a coherent overall concept has yet to be found.

Spaziergang durch das historische Tiergartenviertel
Bewohner – Häuser – Plätze

A Walk through the Historic Tiergarten District
Inhabitants – Houses – Squares

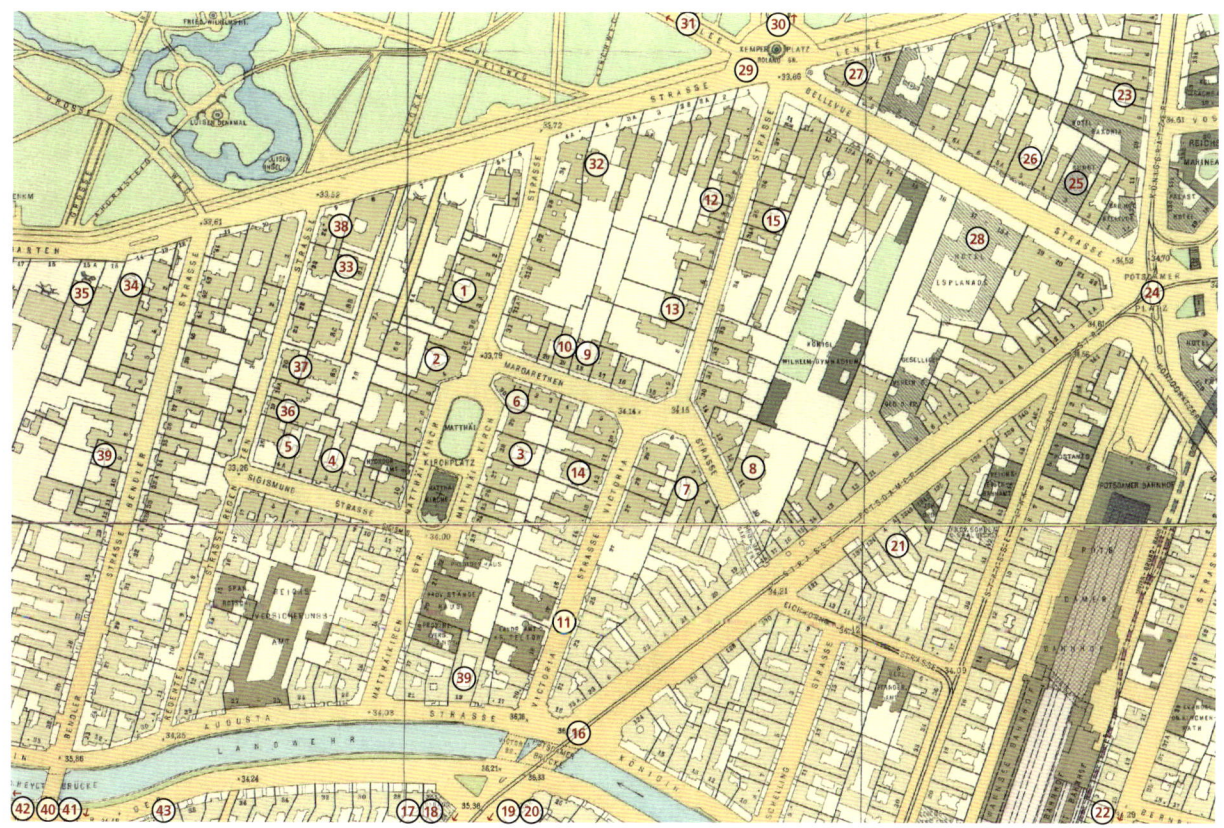

Der Stadtplan von 1910 ist groß in der vorderen Innenklappe dieses Buchs abgedruckt. Die eingetragenen Nummern verweisen auf die Wohnadressen der im Folgenden vorgestellten Persönlichkeiten.

The city map of 1910 is printed large in the front inside flap of this book. The registered numbers indicate the residential adresses of the personalities presented in the following.

1 Matthäikirchstraße 3a
Oscar Huldschinsky

Oscar Huldschinsky (1846–1931), Großindustrieller, besaß eine sehr umfangreiche und qualitativ herausragende Sammlung an Skulpturen, Kunstgewerbe und Gemälden mit dem Schwerpunkt Alte Meister, die neben einem Raffael, dem einzigen in einer deutschen Privatsammlung, Gemälde von Frans Hals, Rembrandt, Rubens, Botticelli und Tiepolo sowie ein Bild Sebastiano del Piombos enthielt.[1] Bei der Auswahl ließ er sich von Wilhelm von Bode (1845–1929, geadelt 1914) beraten, dieser publizierte die Sammlung 1909 in einem Prachtband. Oscar Huldschinsky stiftete den Berliner Museen eine Reihe von Kunstwerken, so der Nationalgalerie Edgar Degas' Gemälde *Die Unterhaltung* und Auguste Rodins Plastik *Der Denker*.

Oscar Huldschinsky (1846–1931), an industrialist, owned a large and important collection of sculpture, paintings and decorative artworks. The assemblage focused on old masters and included not merely the only Raffael in private ownership in Germany but also works by Frans Hals, Rembrandt, Rubens, Botticelli, Tiepolo and Sebastiano del Piombo.[1] When acquiring pictures he was advised by Wilhelm von Bode (1845–1929, ennobled 1914), who published an ornate volume in 1909 detailing the contents of the collection. Oscar Huldschinsky donated a number of artworks to the Berlin Museums. They included Edgar Degas' *The Conversation* and Auguste Rodin's sculpture *The Thinker*, both of which went to the Nationalgalerie (National Gallery).

Matthäikirchstraße 3a. Das Haus wurde von den Architekten Heinrich Kayser und Karl von Großheim im Auftrag von Oscar Huldschinsky errichtet, der hier ab 1893 wohnte.

Matthäikirchstraße 3a. Commissioned by Oscar Huldschinsky, who lived here from 1893 onwards. Built by Heinrich Kayser and Karl von Großheim.

2 Matthäikirchstraße 4
Ernst Curtius und Julius Elias

Ernst Curtius (1814–96), Althistoriker und Klassischer Archäologe, leitete zwischen 1875 und 1881 die deutschen Ausgrabungen im griechischen Olympia. Seine Frau Clara (1828–1900) empfing seit den 1870er-Jahren in der gemeinsamen Wohnung Gelehrte, Diplomaten und Militärs, die sich hier in einer Art Salon regelmäßig trafen. Reinhold Lepsius, *Ernst Curtius*, Öl auf Leinwand, 1891.

Ernst Curtius (1814–96), ancient historian and classical archaeologist, led German excavations in Olympia, Greece, between 1875 and 1881. From the 1870s onwards his wife Clara (1828–1900) hosted a regular salon attracting scholars, diplomats and military personnel. Reinhold Lepsius, *Ernst Curtius*, oil on canvas, 1891.

Julius Elias (1861–1927), hier in seinem Arbeitszimmer, war ein vielseitig begabter Mann: Als Schriftsteller verfasste er unter anderem eine Biografie über Max Liebermann, als Kunstsammler besaß er als einer der ersten eine umfangreiche Sammlung französischer Impressionisten, als Übersetzer war er Mitherausgeber der deutschen Ibsen-Ausgabe und als Kunsthistoriker unterrichtete er an der Technischen Hochschule Charlottenburg.

Julius Elias (1861–1927), shown here in his study, was a polymath whose published works included a biography of Max Liebermann. He was one of the first art connoisseurs to own a large collection of French Impressionist paintings, as a translator he was co-publisher of the German-language Ibsen editions and he taught History of Art at the Technische Hochschule Charlottenburg.

Matthäikirchstraße 4. Das Haus, welches sich rechts im Vordergrund befindet, wurde zwischen 1869 und 1871 im Auftrag des Geheimen Regierungsrats Dr. Wilhelm Stieber als viergeschossiges Mietshaus mit zwei Seitenflügeln von dem Büro Löblich & Sohn errichtet. Abbildung von 1939.

Matthäikirchstraße 4. Built in 1869–1971 by Löblich & Son as a commission from Privy Councillor Dr. Wilhelm Stieber, the residence (front right) was a four-floor rental property with two side wings. Photograph 1939.

3 Matthäikirchstraße 28
Hedwig Dohm

Hedwig Dohm (1831–1919) führte zunächst gemeinsam mit ihrem Mann, dem Schriftsteller und Redakteur des *Kladderadatsch* Ernst Dohm (1819–83), in der Potsdamer Straße eine Art Salon. Nach dem Tod ihres Mannes setzte Hedwig Dohm die Gesellschaften fort, seit 1905 in der Tiergartenstraße, die zumeist von Schriftstellern und Anhängern der Frauenbewegung frequentiert wurden.

Hedwig Dohm (1831–1919) hosted a form of salon on Potsdamer Straße with her husband, the writer and editor of *Kladderadatsch* Ernst Dohm (1819–83). Following the death of her husband Hedwig Dohm continued to organise the gatherings, shifting the venue in 1905 to Tiergartenstraße. The salons drew writers and supporters of the women's movement.

Matthäikirchstraße 28. Das Haus wurde 1862/63 als viergeschossiges Mietshaus errichtet und in den Jahren 1895 und 1903 erweitert. Hedwig Dohm zog 1883 nach dem Tod ihres Mannes Ernst zunächst in eine Wohnung unter dieser Adresse.

Matthäikirchstraße 28. The house was erected as a four-storey rental property in 1862/63 and extended in 1895 and 1903. Hedwig Dohm moved into quarters here in 1883 following the death of her husband, Ernst.

4 Sigismundstraße 3
Adolph von Menzel

Adolph von Menzel in seinem Atelier, 1895.

Adolph von Menzel in his studio, 1895.

Adolph von Menzel (1815–1905, geadelt 1898), Maler, Zeichner und Illustrator. Menzel wurde mit seinen Zeichnungen und Gemälden von Friedrich dem Großen bekannt, die er um das Jahr 1840 zunächst für mehrere Publikationen anfertigte. Sein Werk war sehr vielseitig und brachte ihm ein bedeutendes Renommee, welches sich unter anderem in öffentlichen Ehrungen und Ordensauszeichnungen, der Wahl zum Mitglied der Königlichen Akademie der Künste und der Verleihung einer Professur, die er jedoch nicht wahrnahm, äußerte.

Adolph von Menzel (1815–1905, ennobled 1898), painter, sketcher and illustrator. Menzel came to prominence with his drawings and paintings of Friedrich der Große, produced in or around 1840 and aimed at a number of publications. He was a versatile artist and became a household name because of it. This in turn was reflected in a raft of public awards and accolades, his election to the Royal Academy of Arts and the bestowment of a professorship, which latter he did not take up.

Sigismundstraße 3. Hier (das mittlere Gebäude in nebenstehender Darstellung) befand sich ein um 1864 errichtetes, viergeschossiges Mietshaus, in dem Adolph von Menzel seit 1890 lebte und arbeitete. Vermieter von Menzel war ab 1898 Eduard Arnhold, dieser hatte das Gebäude mitsamt des umgebenden Grundstücks mit dem Ziel erworben, die Bebauungsgrenze für einen Galeriebau auf seinem benachbarten Grundstück in der Regentenstraße 19 zu erweitern.

Sigismundstraße 3. This (middle building in the picture on the right) was the site of a four-storey rental property, constructed in 1864. Adolph von Menzel lived and worked here from 1890 onwards. Menzel's landlord was Eduard Arnhold, who had purchased the building and plot in 1898 with a view to extending the building-land boundary to make room for a gallery on his neighbouring property at Regentenstraße 19.

5 Sigismundstraße 4a
Paul Parey

Nach dem Tod des Verlegers **Paul Parey** (1842–1900) kaufte der Bankier Wilhelm Kopetzky (1847–1924) die Villa, die aber noch heute nach ihrem ersten Besitzer benannt wird. Zu sehen ist vermutlich die Familie Kopetzky beim Kaffee im Jahr 1903.

The banker Wilhelm Kopetzky (1847–1924) bought the villa following the death of its first owner, the publisher **Paul Parey** (1842–1900). The house still bears his name. The photo presumably shows the Kopetzky family taking coffee, 1903.

Sigismundstraße 4a. Das Gebäude wurde 1895/96 für den Verleger Paul Parey nach einem Entwurf des Architekturbüros Heinrich Kayser und Karl von Großheim als Einfamilienhaus erbaut. Heute ist die Villa in die Gemäldegalerie integriert.

Sigismundstraße 4a. The building was built as a single, detached dwelling in 1895/96 for the publisher Paul Parey to designs by the architecture office of Heinrich Kayser and Karl von Großheim. Today the villa forms part of Gemäldegalerie.

6 Margaretenstraße 1
Tilla Durieux

Tilla Durieux (1880–1971), eigentlich Ottilie Godeffroy, Schauspielerin. Nach ihrer Schauspielausbildung in Wien kam Tilla Durieux 1903 nach Berlin an das Deutsche Theater und spielte bis zu ihrer Emigration 1933 an allen großen Bühnen der Stadt. Zudem erhielt sie 1914 ihre erste Filmrolle, es folgten bis 1970 zahlreiche weitere. Zwischen 1910 und 1926 war sie mit dem Galeristen und Verleger Paul Cassirer verheiratet.

Tilla Durieux (1880–1971), the stage name of the actress Ottilie Godeffroy. After completing her drama training in Vienna, Tilla Durieux joined the Deutsches Theater in Berlin, acting on all the major stages up until her emigration in 1933. Her first film role came in 1914, her last in 1970. She was married to the gallery owner and publisher Paul Cassirer between 1910 and 1926.

Tilla Durieux als Zarin Katharina in *Spielereien einer Kaiserin* von Max Dauthendey, um 1911.

Tilla Durieux as Czarina Catherine in *Spielereien einer Kaiserin* by Max Dauthendey, ca. 1911.

Margaretenstraße 1. In den Jahren 1868 bis 1869 zusammen mit der Matthäikirchstraße 30 als viergeschossiges Mietshaus errichtetes Eckgebäude. Der Architekt Carl Wilhelm Bühling war hier Bauherr und Architekt in einer Person. Tilla Durieux zog nach ihrer Hochzeit mit Paul Cassirer in die Margaretenstraße 1, in der ihr Mann bereits lebte. Das Ehepaar blieb hier bis 1915 wohnen, danach bezog es das neu erworbene Haus in der Victoriastraße 35.

Margaretenstraße 1. A four-storey rental property built on the corner of Margareten- and Matthäikirchstraße. Architect Carl Wilhelm Bühling was also the owner. Tilla Durieux moved into Margaretenstraße 1 after her marriage to Paul Cassirer, who was already living there. They stayed here until 1915, when they shifted to newly purchased quarters at Victoriastraße 35.

7 Margaretenstraße 7
Marie von Olfers

Marie von Olfers (1826–1924), Schriftstellerin und Malerin, Tochter des Generaldirektors der Königlichen Museen Ignaz von Olfers, war zunächst in den Salon ihrer Mutter Hedwig eingebunden. Ab 1892 empfing sie eigenständig unter wechselnden Adressen in der Margareten-, Victoria- und Regentenstraße sowie ab 1910 am Schöneberger Ufer einmal wöchentlich vor allem Schriftsteller, Musiker, Kunsthistoriker und Bildende Künstler wie Mitglieder der Familie Begas, Georg Kolbe, Harry Graf Kessler, Franz und Frieda von Lipperheide oder Rainer Maria Rilke.[2] Hier zu sehen in ihrem Salon, vermutlich 1923/24.

Marie von Olfers (1826–1924), writer and painter, daughter of Ignaz von Olfers, Director General of the Royal Museums, was involved first in her mother Hedwig's salon. From 1892 onwards she held her own gatherings in the Margaretenstraße, Victoriastraße and Regentenstraße and, from 1910, on Schöneberger Ufer. Her weekly salons attracted primarily writers, musicians, art historians and fine artists such as members of the Begas family, Georg Kolbe, Harry Graf Kessler, Franz and Frieda von Lipperheide and Rainer Maria Rilke.[2] The photograph shows Marie von Olfers in her salon, presumably 1923/24.

Margaretenstraße 7. Das Gebäude wurde 1861/62 für den Bildhauer August Julius Streichenberg (1814–78) als Mietshaus errichtet. Laut dem Berliner Adressbuch war Marie von Olfers hier gemeinsam mit ihrer Mutter Hedwig gemeldet, nach deren Tod im Jahr 1891 wohnte sie noch bis 1896 unter dieser Adresse. Die Aufnahme stammt von 1931.

Margaretenstraße 7. The building was erected in 1861/62 as a rental property for the sculptor August Julius Streichenberg (1814–78). According to the Berlin address book, the property was home to Marie von Olfers until 1896 and her mother Hedwig until 1891. The photograph was taken in 1931.

8 Margaretenstraße 11
Willibald von Dirksen

Willibald von Dirksen (1852–1928, geadelt 1887) war als Jurist im Auswärtigen Amt tätig und Mitglied des Abgeordnetenhauses. Dirksen besaß eine umfangreiche Kunstsammlung mit einigen Gemälden und zahlreichen kunsthandwerklichen Arbeiten vor allem der italienischen Hochrenaissance, die er auf Anraten Wilhelm von Bodes zusammenstellte. Abgebildet ist das Speisezimmer im Haus Dirksen.

Willibald von Dirksen (1852–1928, ennobled 1887) was a lawyer in the Foreign Office and a Member of Parliament. Dirksen owned a large collection of arts and crafts and some paintings, in particular from the Italian High Renaissance. He was assisted in his acquisitions by Wilhelm von Bode. The photograph shows the dining room in Dirksen's home.

Margaretenstraße 11. In die Ausstattung der 1894/95 im Auftrag von Willibald von Dirksen durch das Architekturbüro Heinrich Kayser und Karl von Großheim erbauten Villa waren kostbare historische Deckenverkleidungen und Kamine integriert.

Margaretenstraße 11. Commissioned by Willibald von Dirksen and built in 1894/95 to plans by the architects Heinrich Kayser and Karl von Großheim, the villa featured precious, historical ceiling linings and fireplaces.

9 Margaretenstraße 18
Ludwig Hoffmann

Ludwig Hoffmann (1852–1932), Architekt, prägte als Stadtbaurat die Stadt Berlin mit mehr als 400 öffentlichen Gebäuden, darunter zahlreiche Schulen, Krankenhäuser, das Märkische Museum, das Stadthaus am Alexanderplatz und der Märchenbrunnen im Volkspark Friedrichshain. Von seinem Freund Alfred Messel (1853–1909) übernahm Hoffmann nach dessen Tod die Weiterführung des Pergamonmuseums. Zuvor hatten beide zwischen 1896 und 1905 gemeinsam in dem Mietshaus Potsdamer Straße 121 d gewohnt. Hoffmanns Ehefrau Marie, geb. Weisbach, war die Tochter von Valentin Weisbach (1843–99), sie wuchs in unmittelbarer Nähe in dem von ihrem Vater gebauten Haus in der Tiergartenstraße 4 auf.

Ludwig Hoffmann (1852–1932), architect and councillor for public works, was instrumental in the construction of over 400 public buildings in Berlin. They included schools, hospitals, the Märkisches Museum, the Stadthaus at Alexanderplatz and the Märchenbrunnen in the Volkspark Friedrichshain. Hoffmann took over directorship of the Pergamonmuseum from his friend, Alfred Messel (1853–1909). The two men had previously lived in rented quarters at Potsdamer Straße 121 d between 1896 and 1905. Hoffmann's wife Marie, née Weisbach, was the daughter of Valentin Weisbach (1843–99) and grew up in the house close-by built by her father at Tiergartenstraße 4.

Margaretenstraße 18. Das Gebäude wurde 1858 für einen Bankier errichtet, später wohnte hier bis zu seinem Tod 1899 der Politiker Ludwig Bamberger. Danach erwarb Valentin Weisbach das Haus, aus dessen Nachlass erhielten es Marie und Ludwig Hoffmann, die es um ein Geschoss erweiterten und 1905 einzogen.

Margaretenstraße 18. The building was erected for a banker in 1858 and was the residence of the politician Ludwig Bamberger until his death in 1899. It was then purchased by Valentin Weisbach, who bequeathed it to Marie and Ludwig Hoffmann, who in turn added a storey and moved in in 1905.

10 Margaretenstraße 19
Werner Weisbach

Werner Weisbach (1873–1953), Kunsthistoriker, absolvierte zunächst ein Volontariat im (Alten) Museum und arbeitete unter Wilhelm von Bode in der Abteilung für Malerei und Skulptur, 1926 erhielt er schließlich eine Professur an der Friedrich-Wilhelms-Universität. Weisbach erbte die Kunstsammlung seines Vaters Valentin und erweiterte diese, ebenso führte er die Bestrebungen des Vaters im sozialen Wohnungsbau fort.

Werner Weisbach (1873–1953), art historian, began his career with an unpaid position at the Altes Museum (Old Museum) and worked under Wilhelm von Bode in the painting and sculpture department. In 1926 he finally took a professorship at the Friedrich Wilhelm University. Weisbach inherited and extended his father Valentin's art collection and also sought to continue the work done by his father to improve social housing.

Margaretenstraße 19. Den Bauplatz erhielt Werner Weisbach aus dem Erbe seines Vaters, als Architekt engagierte er seinen Schwager Peter Dybwad (1859–1921). Dieser hatte zuvor mit seinem Studienfreund Ludwig Hoffmann den Auftrag für das Reichsgericht in Leipzig erhalten und war als dessen Mitarbeiter an der Ausführung beteiligt. Die Vorgabe Weisbachs an Dybwad für das Aussehen des Hauses war: eine schlichte Fassade, die an den Stil französischer Hôtels des 17. Jahrhunderts erinnert, mit hohen Fenstern im Hauptstockwerk zur möglichst guten Beleuchtung der Kunstgegenstände.

Margaretenstraße 19. Werner Weisbach inherited the site was from his father and hired his brother in-law, Peter Dybwad (1859–1921), as architect. Dybwad had previously been commissioned with his college friend Ludwig Hoffmann to build the imperial court in Leipzig and was involved in the realisation of the project as Hoffmann's colleague. Weisbach's instructions to Dybwad were to deliver a plain façade reminiscent of a 17th-century French hôtels, with tall windows on the main floor, the better to illuminate the artworks.

11 Victoriastraße

Wohnhäuser in der Victoriastraße, errichtet von Friedrich Hitzig (1811–81) in den Jahren 1855 bis 1860, Lithografie um 1860. Die obere Reihe zeigt die Häuser Nummern 9, 8–7 und 6–5, die untere die Nummern 9a, 34, 33 und 30.

Residences on Victoriastraße, built by Friedrich Hitzig (1811–81) between 1855 and 1860. Lithography ca. 1860. The top row shows house numbers 9, 8–7 and 6–5, the bottom row 9a, 34, 33 and 30.

Kreuzung Victoria- und Margaretenstraße, Blick in den westlichen Teil der Margaretenstraße, um 1900. Links ist zu sehen die Victoriastraße 10 (1858–59), rechts die Nr. 9 (1857), beide von Friedrich Hitzig.

The intersection at Victoriastraße and Margaretenstraße. View west down Margaretenstraße, ca. 1900. On the left: Victoriastraße 10 (1858–59); on the right: No. 9 (1857), both were erected by Friedrich Hitzig.

12 Victoriastraße 3–4
Emil Rathenau

Max Liebermann, *Bildnisstudie Emil Rathenau*, Öl auf Pappe, 1907.

Max Liebermann, *study for a portrait of Emil Rathenau*, oil on cardboard, 1907.

Emil Rathenau (1838–1915), Maschinenbauingenieur und Unternehmer. Nachdem Rathenau 1882 die Rechte zur Nutzung der Patente von Thomas Edison für Deutschland erhalten hatte, gründete er 1883 das Unternehmen, welches ab 1887 als Allgemeine Elektricitäts-Gesellschaft (AEG) firmierte. Emil Rathenau war ein Cousin Max Liebermanns und ein enger Freund Eduard Arnholds. Seit 1912 ließ er sich krankheitsbedingt durch seinen Sohn Walther Rathenau (1867–1922) vertreten, nach dem Tod des Vaters erhielt der Sohn das Präsidium der AEG. Walther Rathenau war neben seiner Arbeit für die AEG auch als Schriftsteller tätig und als Politiker bekannt, Anfang 1922 übernahm er bis zu seiner Ermordung im Juni des Jahres das Amt des Außenministers.

Emil Rathenau (1838–1915), mechanical engineer and entrepreneur. A year after acquiring the rights on the patents of Thomas Edison for Germany in 1882 Rathenau founded the company that, from 1887 onwards, would be known as Allgemeine Elektricitäts-Gesellschaft (AEG). Emil Rathenau was a cousin of Max Liebermann and a close friend of Eduard Arnhold. Serious illness led him to install his son, Walther Rathenau (1867–1922), as his representative in 1912, Walther assuming presidency of the company on his father's death. In addition to his work for AEG, Walther Rathenau was a writer and politician. From early 1922 until his assassination in June of that year he held the post of Foreign Minister.

Victoriastraße 3−4. Emil Rathenau besaß das Haus in der Victoriastraße 3 bereits seit den 1860er-Jahren, von 1901 bis 1910 wohnte hier sein Sohn Walther. 1911 ließ Emil Rathenau das Gebäude Nr. 3 ebenso wie das Haus Nr. 4, das er kurz zuvor gekauft hatte, abreißen und einen Neubau errichten, in dem er bis zu seinem Tod wohnte. Danach ist als Eigentümer Walther Rathenau eingetragen, es lebte dort aber dessen Mutter Mathilde Rathenau.

Victoriastraße 3−4. Emil Rathenau acquired the house in the 1860s, his son Walther living here from 1901 to 1910. In 1911 Emil Rathenau had No. 3 demolished along with No. 4, which he had bought shortly before, to make way for a new home, where he lived until his death. The house passed to Walther Rathenau but was occupied by his mother Mathilde.

13 Victoriastraße 7
Eduard Simon

Eduard Simon (1864–1929), Teilhaber der Baumwoll- und Leinenfabrik Gebr. Simon, Vetter von James Simon (1851–1932). Simon sammelte neben europäischer Renaissancemalerei viele europäische Gemälde des 18. Jahrhunderts sowie zahlreiche kunstgewerbliche Arbeiten.[3] Er verließ sich beim Aufbau seiner Sammlung auf Wilhelm von Bode. Zum Dank stiftete er den Museen eine Reihe von Kunstwerken. Auf der Abbildung ist Simons Arbeitszimmer zu sehen.

Eduard Simon (1864–1929), partner in the Gebr. Simon cotton and linen factory and cousin of James Simon (1851–1932). Eduard Simon collected paintings from the European Renaissance, numerous European paintings from the 18th century and a large body of decorative arts.[3] He relied on recommendations from Wilhelm von Bode when adding to his collection. In recognition of this assistance, he donated artworks to the Berlin Museums. The photograph shows Simon's study.

Victoriastraße 7. Das Haus ließ Eduard Simon von Alfred Messel 1902/03 gezielt planen, um eine Reihe von Kunstwerken seiner Sammlung, die er zu diesem Zweck erworben hatte, zu integrieren. So waren zum Beispiel im Speisezimmer ein Deckengemälde und Grisaillen von Giovanni Battista Tiepolo zu sehen und im Salon ein venezianisches Spiegelkabinett im Rokokostil, welches er mit französischen Möbeln aus der Zeit Ludwigs XV. präsentierte.

Victoriastraße 7. Eduard Simon had this house built by Alfred Messel in 1902/03 to house a series of artworks that he had purchased for this purpose. The dining room boasted a ceiling fresco and grisailles by Giovanni Battista Tiepolo and the drawing room featured a rococo-style Venetian hall of mirrors complete with Louis Quinze furniture.

14 Victoriastraße 12
Ernst Eberhard von Ihne

Ernst Eberhard von Ihne (1848–1917), Hofarchitekt und Sammler. Nach seinen Plänen entstanden in Berlin unter anderem das Kaiser-Friedrich-Museum (heute Bodemuseum) und die Staatsbibliothek Unter den Linden. Teile seiner Kunstsammlung integrierte Ihne in die Ausstattung seines Hauses, so waren an mehreren Orten alte italienische Kamine eingebaut.[4] Außerdem befanden sich im Musikzimmer vier große Grisaillen von Giambattista Tiepolo.

Ernst Eberhard von Ihne (1848–1917), court architect and collector. The Kaiser Friedrich Museum (today's Bode Museum) and the State Library Unter den Linden were built to his plans. Ihne incorporated some items from his art collection into his house, including several Italian fireplaces.[4] The music room also featured four large grisailles by Giambattista Tiepolo.

Victoriastraße 12 (hier das zurückgesetzte Haus in der Mitte). Errichtet wurde das Gebäude in den Jahren 1855–60 von Friedrich Hitzig als Mietshaus. Ernst von Ihne kaufte es im Jahr 1905 und zog nach Umbauten mit seiner Familie ein Jahr später hier ein – einzige Bedingung für den Kauf war, dass die Vorbesitzerin in den 12 Zimmern des Erdgeschosses als Mieterin wohnen bleiben durfte.

Victoriastraße 12 (the recessed house in the middle). The building was built in 1855–60 by Friedrich Hitzig to house tenants. Ernst von Ihne bought it in 1905 and moved in with his family a year later. The only condition of sale was that the previous owner would be allowed to continue to rent the 12 rooms on the ground floor.

15 Victoriastraße 35
Paul Cassirer

Paul Cassirer (1871–1926) eröffnete gemeinsam mit seinem Vetter Bruno Cassirer (1872–1941) 1898 einen Verlag und eine Kunsthandlung. Nach Differenzen lösten beide die Zusammenarbeit 1901 wieder auf. Bruno Cassirer übernahm den Verlag und verließ die Victoriastraße, Paul Cassirer blieb mit der Kunsthandlung, in der er, eng verbunden mit der Berliner Secession, erfolgreich moderne französische und deutsche Künstler vertrat. 1908 gründete Paul Cassirer zudem in der gegenüberliegenden Victoriastraße 5 einen eigenen Verlag.

In 1898 **Paul Cassirer** (1871–1926) and his cousin Bruno Cassirer (1872–1941) opened a publishing house and art dealership. After the partnership was wound up in 1901 following differences Bruno Cassirer took over the publishing house and left Victoriastraße, while Paul retained the art dealership and went on to prosper as an agent for French and German artists, closely linked to the Berliner Secession. In 1908 Paul Cassirer created his own publishing house across the road at Victoriastraße 5.

Leopold von Kalckreuth, *Paul Cassirer*, o. J.

Leopold von Kalckreuth, *Paul Cassirer*, undated.

Victoriastraße 35. Das Gebäude wurde 1839 von dem Maurermeister Carl Ludwig Schüttler und dem Ratszimmermeister Johann Ludwig Schultz als dreigeschossiges Wohnhaus errichtet. Ab 1898 waren Bruno und Paul Cassirer hier Mieter, ihre Räume ließen sie zum Teil durch den belgischen Architekten und Designer Henry van de Velde einrichten. Im Jahr 1899 entstand als Erweiterungsbau im Garten des Grundstücks die hier abgebildete provisorische Kunsthalle. Nachdem Paul Cassirer 1910 Haus und Grundstück erworben hatte, ließ er 1912 einen neuen Oberlichtsaal einrichten.

Victoriastraße 35. Constructed in 1839 by master builder Carl Ludwig Schüttler and master carpenter Johann Ludwig Schultz as a three-storey residence. From 1898 onwards Bruno and Paul Cassirer were tenants, and they contracted Belgian architect and designer Henry van de Velde to furnish their rooms. In 1899 an annexe was built in the garden to be used as a temporary art gallery, shown here. Two years after acquiring the property in 1910, Paul Cassirer had a new hall with skylights erected.

16 Potsdamer Brücke / Potsdamer Straße

Die **Potsdamer Brücke** über den Landwehrkanal und die neue Potsdamer Straße in der Bildmitte. Links davon die sich im Bau befindliche Neue Nationalgalerie, rechts die von Bäumen gesäumte alte Potsdamer Straße, die noch über das Gelände der später dort errichteten Staatsbibliothek führt, 1967.

Potsdamer Bridge over the Landwehrkanal with the new Potsdamer Straße in the middle. On the left hand side the New National Gallery, under construction, on the right the tree-lined old Potsdamer Straße still running across the area where the National Library will later be built, 1967.

Landwehrkanal, Luftbildaufnahme von 1919. Bei der rechten der beiden über den Kanal verlaufenden Straßen handelt es sich um die Potsdamer Straße mit der Potsdamer Brücke, die linke ist die Victoriastraße, die an der Victoriabrücke endet. Das offene Dreieck zwischen den Brücken war als „Spucknapf" bekannt. An der oberen Kanalseite ist die Königin-Augusta-Straße zu sehen (heute Reichpietschufer), an der unteren das Schöneberger Ufer.

The Landwehrkanal, an aerial photo from 1919. Potsdamer Straße crosses the canal at Potsdamer Bridge on the right; Victoriastraße ends at Victoria Bridge on the left. The triangle between the two bridges was known as the "spittoon". Königin-Augusta-Straße (today Reichpietschufer) runs along the canal's northern bank, on the other is Schöneberger Ufer.

16 Potsdamer Brücke / Potsdamer Straße

Potsdamer Brücke mit Blick in die Potsdamer Straße, 2015.

Potsdamer Bridge, view into Potsdamer Straße, 2015.

Die **Potsdamer Brücke** (links) und die Victoriabrücke (rechts) mit dem „Spucknapf" in der Mitte. Blick in die Potsdamer Straße, um 1900.

Potsdamer Bridge (left) and Victoria Bridge (right) with the "spittoon" in the middle. View into Potsdamer Straße, ca. 1900.

17 Potsdamer Straße 38
Franz von Lipperheide

Franz von Lipperheide (1838–1906), Verleger und Sammler, gab gemeinsam mit seiner Frau Frieda (1840–96) mehrere Zeitschriften zu den Themen Mode, Unterhaltung und Kostümkunde heraus. Der finanzielle Erfolg des Verlages ermöglichte es dem Ehepaar, eine umfangreiche Sammlung an Vorlagenwerken, Gemälden, Grafiken und Literatur über Mode und Kleidung, Materialkunde und verarbeitete Techniken zusammenzutragen. Die Sammlung befindet sich heute zum größten Teil in der Kunstbibliothek und der Gemäldegalerie.

Franz von Lipperheide (1838–1906), publisher and collector, and his wife Frieda (1840–96) published several journals on the subjects of fashion, entertainment and elegant clothing. The financial success of the publishing house allowed the couple to assemble a large collection of pattern books, paintings, drawings and literature devoted to fashion and clothes, materials science and manufacturing techniques. Much of the collection can now be found in the Kunstbibliothek (Art Library) and the Gemäldegalerie (Gallery of Old Masters).

Potsdamer Straße 38. Franz und Frieda von Lipperheide erwarben das Haus 1874 und bewohnten es bis zu ihrem Tod. Frieda von Lipperheide, die unter anderen eng mit Julius Lessing (1843–1908), dem Direktor des Berliner Kunstgewerbemuseums zusammenarbeitete, hielt hier auch einen literarischen Salon ab, in dem sich Künstler, Gelehrte, Musiker und Schriftsteller trafen.

Potsdamer Straße 38. Franz and Frieda von Lipperheide bought this house in 1874 and lived here until their deaths. Frieda von Lipperheide, who also had a close professional association with, among other personages, Julius Lessing (1843–1908), Director of Berlin's Kunstgewerbemuseum (Museum of Decorative Arts), hosted a literary salon here that was popular among artists, scholars, musicians and writers.

18 Potsdamer Straße 113, Villa IV
Anton von Werner

Anton von Werner im Kostüm als „Faust", o. J.
Anton von Werner in "Faust" costume, undated.

Anton von Werner (1843–1915) malte im öffentlichen Auftrag zahlreiche historische Ereignisse und porträtierte regelmäßig die politischen und gesellschaftlichen Größen der Zeit. Er war einer der erfolgreichsten und zugleich umstrittensten Maler des Kaiserreichs, der in engem Kontakt zum Königshaus stand und mit Orden und Auszeichnungen überhäuft wurde. Er erhielt einflussreiche Posten, so war er seit 1875 Direktor der neu gebildeten Lehranstalt der Preußischen Akademie der Wissenschaft, der Hochschule für bildende Künste. Außerdem stand er mit zwei Unterbrechungen von 1887 bis 1907 dem Verein Berliner Künstler vor, der sich in dieser Zeit konservativer ausrichtete und neuen Einfluss gewann, weil ihm beachtliche Mittel zur Verfügung gestellt wurden.

Anton von Werner (1843–1915) captured numerous historic events on canvas, working to commissions, and was often to be found painting the portraits of major political and social figures of the day. He was one of the most successful yet controversial painters of the German Empire, moving in circles very close to royalty and the recipient of multiple medals and awards. He was appointed to influential posts, one of which was his directorship of the newly formed school within the Prussian Academy of Sciences, the College of Fine Arts, a position that he held from 1875 until his death. He also chaired the Society of Berlin Artists from 1887 to 1907, with two breaks in his incumbency. The Society became more conservative during von Werner's administration and gained in influence as a result of the large amount of funding that it received.

Potsdamer Straße 113, Villa IV. Anton von Werner ließ das Gebäude 1873 (hier: Musikzimmer) von dem Architekten Ernst Klingenberg als zweigeschossiges Wohn- und Atelierhaus errichten. 1881 erweiterte von Werner die Villa um einen Seitenflügel, 1884 das Atelier im Obergeschoss um weitere Räume. Das Haus, welches heute noch unter der Adresse Potsdamer Straße 81 a erhalten ist, wurde nach dem Tod des Malers mehrfach aufgestockt und nachträglich verputzt.

Potsdamer Straße 113, Villa IV. Anton von Werner commissioned architect Ernst Klingenberg to build this two-storey residential and studio property in 1873 (here: the music room). Von Werner added a side wing in 1881 and more rooms to the top-floor studio in 1884. Still in existence today at Potsdamer Straße 81 a, the house had floors added on a number of occasions after the death of the painter and also received a mantle of plaster.

19 Potsdamer Straße 118 b
Kunstsalon Keller & Reiner

Georges Lemmen, Briefbogen für Keller & Reiner, Akzidenzdruck, um 1910.

Georges Lemmen, printed notepaper for Keller & Reiner, job printing, ca. 1910.

Louis Oppenheim, „Eröffnung des neuerbauten Ausstellungshauses Potsdamer Straße 118 b Anfang November", Plakat, um 1910.

Louis Oppenheim, "Opening of the new auction house at Potsdamer Straße 118 b, early November", poster, ca. 1910.

Im Jahr 1897 gründeten der Innenarchitekt **Martin Keller** und **Carl R. Reiner** zunächst in der Potsdamer Straße 122 einen nach ihnen benannten Kunstsalon. Spezialisiert waren sie neben einer Abteilung für moderne Kunst vor allem auf die Ausstellung und den Verkauf zeitgenössischen Kunstgewerbes. 1908 trennten sich die Partner. Carl R. Reiner eröffnete mit Karl Lewinsky einen neuen Salon, der unter dem alten Namen weiterlief und in die Potsdamer Straße 118 b umzog. Spätestens ab 1911 fanden hier auch Auktionen statt. An dem erfolgreichen Beispiel Keller & Reiner orientierten sich in Berlin in kurzer Zeit derart viele Kunsthändler, dass sich der Verkauf kunstgewerblicher Güter bald als eigenes Marktsegment etablierte und Berlin noch vor dem Ersten Weltkrieg deutschlandweit zu *dem* Handelsplatz für angewandte Kunst wurde.

In 1897 interior designer **Martin Keller** and **Carl R. Reiner** created their eponymous art salon at Potsdamer Straße 122. Besides their section on modern art, the pair focussed particularly on exhibiting and selling contemporary decorative arts. The partnership broke up in 1908, but Carl R. Reiner opened a new salon with Karl Lewinsky, moving the venue to Potsdamer Straße 118 b but retaining the original name. Auctions were being held here by 1911. So many art dealers emerged in Berlin, eager to emulate the success of Keller & Reiner, that the sale of arts and crafts soon formed its own market segment, turning Berlin into the trading hotspot for applied arts throughout the country prior to the First World War.

Potsdamer Straße 118 b. Von dem Architekten Bruno Schmitz gestaltetes Foyer des Kunstsalons Keller & Reiner, um 1910.

Potsdamer Straße 118 b. The foyer of the Keller & Reiner art salon, designed by architect Bruno Schmitz, ca. 1910.

20 Potsdamer Straße 122 a
Rudolph Lepke's Kunstauktionshaus

Rudolph Lepke's Kunstauktionshaus. Rudolph Lepke (1845–1904) entstammte einer Kunsthändlerfamilie, er gründete 1869 zunächst in der Kochstraße das erste Kunstauktionshaus in Berlin. Hier fanden spektakuläre Versteigerungen statt, so 1887 der Verkauf von 1.062 Gemälden der Berliner Nationalgalerie, die Lepke mit dem befreundeten Wilhelm von Bode vorbereitet hatte. Rudolph Lepke war selbst Kunstsammler und förderte unter anderem das Hohenzollernmuseum im Schloss Monbijou. Nachdem Rudolph Lepke schwer erkrankt war, übernahmen 1900 seine Mitarbeiter, die Brüder Adolf und Gustav Wolffenberg sowie Hans Carl Krüger, das Geschäft.

Rudolph Lepke's art auction house. Rudolph Lepke (1845–1904) was born into a family of art dealers. He founded Berlin's first art auction house in 1869, located initially on Kochstraße. This was the scene of spectacular auctions. In 1887 the house auctioned off 1,062 paintings from the inventory of Berlin's Nationalgalerie, an event prepared by Lepke and his friend Wilhelm von Bode. Rudolph Lepke was an art collector in his own right and supported a number of institutions, among them the Hohenzollern Museum in Monbijou Palace. In 1900, with Rudolph Lepke seriously ill, his colleagues – brothers Adolf and Gustav Wolffenberg and Hans Carl Krüger – took over operations.

Potsdamer Straße 122a. 1912 zog das Auktionshaus in einen Neubau in die Potsdamer Straße 122 a/122 b, den die Besitzer bei dem Architekten Adolf Wollenberg in Auftrag gegeben hatten.

Potsdamer Straße 122a. In 1912 the auction house moved to newly built premises at Potsdamer Straße 122 a/122 b, built by the architect Adolf Wollenberg.

21 Potsdamer Straße 134 a
Herwarth Walden

Herwarth Walden mit seiner zweiten Frau Nell in ihrem Speisezimmer in der Potsdamer Straße 134 a, 1916.

Herwarth Walden with his second wife Nell in their dining room in Potsdamer Straße 134 a, 1916.

Herwarth Walden (1878–1941), Schriftsteller, Verleger, Galerist und Komponist. Er gründete 1910 die Zeitschrift *Der Sturm* und 1912 den gleichnamigen Verlag. Herwarth Walden war einer der wichtigsten Förderer der deutschen Avantgarde des frühen 20. Jahrhunderts, in seiner Galerie und dem Verlag unterstützte und vermarktete er viele damals noch wenig bekannte Künstler wie Marc Chagall, August Macke, Wassily Kandinsky, Paul Klee und Gabriele Münter.

Herwarth Walden (1878–1941), writer, publisher, gallery owner and composer. In 1910 he founded the journal *Der Sturm* and, in 1912, the publishing house of the same name. Herwarth Walden was instrumental in promoting the German avant-garde movement of the early 20th century. His gallery and publishing house supported and acted as agent for many artists who would later become famous. They included Marc Chagall, August Macke, Wassily Kandinsky, Paul Klee and Gabriele Münter.

Potsdamer Straße 134 a. Im Frühjahr 1914 stellte Herwarth Walden die Arbeiten Marc Chagalls (1887–1985) erstmals in einer Einzelausstellung in seiner Galerie *Der Sturm* vor, Chagall reiste eigens aus seinem damaligen Wohnort Paris zur Vernissage an.

Potsdamer Straße 134 a. Herwarth Walden showed works by Marc Chagall (1887–1985) in his gallery *Der Sturm* for the first time in the spring of 1914. Chagall travelled from Paris specially to attend the opening.

22 Köthener Straße 28
Harry Graf Kessler

Harry Graf Kessler (1868–1937, geadelt 1879) engagierte sich auf unterschiedlichen kulturellen Ebenen, aber auch in der Politik. Er arbeitete unter anderem seit 1895 als ehrenamtliches Redaktionsmitglied der Kunst- und Literaturzeitschrift *Pan*, übernahm 1903 die ehrenamtliche Leitung des Weimarer Museums für Kunst und Kunstgewerbe und setzte sich für eine Reform des Theaters ein. Mit rund 150 Meisterwerken der Klassischen Moderne – Gemälden, Skulpturen und Grafiken –, die Kessler zwischen 1895 und 1914 erwarb, gehörte er zu den bedeutendsten Privatsammlern und Förderern avantgardistischer Kunst in Deutschland. Bemerkenswert ist außerdem sein literarischer Nachlass in Form eines seit 1880 intensiv geführten Tagebuchs, welches als neunbändige Veröffentlichung des Deutschen Literaturarchivs in Marbach vorliegt.

Harry Graf Kessler (1868–1937, ennobled 1879) was active at a number of cultural levels and also in politics. Among other endeavours he worked as an unpaid editor of *Pan*, the art and literature journal, from 1895 onwards, became honorary head of the Weimar Museum for Arts and Crafts and laboured to achieve reform in the theatre. The 150 Early Modernist masterpieces – paintings, sculptures and drawings – acquired by Kessler between 1895 and 1914 made him one of the most important private collectors and patrons of avant-garde art in Germany. He is also noted for the papers he left behind on his death: from 1880 onwards he kept a detailed diary, which was published as a nine-volume work and is held in the German Literary Archive in Marbach.

Edvard Munch, *Harry Graf Kessler*, Öl auf Leinwand, 1906.

Edvard Munch, *Harry Graf Kessler*, oil on canvas, 1906.

Köthener Straße 28. Seine Wohnung ließ sich Harry Graf Kessler 1897 von Henry van de Velde einrichten, die hier abgebildeten Möbel waren mit weißem Schleiflack gestaltet, integriert ein Gemälde von Georges Seurat aus der Sammlung Kesslers.

Köthener Straße 28. In 1897 Harry Graf Kessler commissioned Henry van de Velde to furnish his flat. The furniture pictured here was sand-papered to a white gloss finish, in the background a painting by Georges Seurat from Kessler's collection.

23 Königgrätzer Straße 8
Hohenzollern-Kunstgewerbehaus

Werbung für das Hohenzollern-Kunstgewerbehaus, Entwurf Julius Gipkens, o. J.

Advertising for the Hohenzollern-Kunstgewerbehaus, designed by Julius Gipkens, undated.

Das Hohenzollern-Kunstgewerbehaus, Inhaber Friedmann & Weber wurde 1879 von Hermann Hirschwald (1849–1906) als Verkaufsstelle für vorbildliches Kunstgewerbe gegründet. Unterstützt wurde Hirschwald von dem preußischen Kronprinzenpaar, das sich sehr für die Reform der angewandten Kunst einsetzte – der Firmenname ist an die beiden monarchischen Fürsprecher angelehnt. 1900/01 vereinte Hirschwald vorrübergehend auch die Werkstätten Henry van de Veldes mit den eigenen. Nach Hirschwalds Tod übernahmen 1906 Ernst Friedmann (1876–unbekannt) und Hermann Weber (1876–1937) das Haus, beide waren zuvor bei Keller & Reiner tätig gewesen und hatten bereits unter dem Namen *Friedmann & Weber Kunstmöbel und Innendekoration* ein Geschäft betrieben.

The Hohenzollern-Kunstgewerbehaus, owned by Friedmann & Weber, was opened in 1879 by Hermann Hirschwald (1849–1906) as an outlet for showpiece decorative arts. Hirschwald was supported in his venture by the royal couple, who were strongly in favour of reform in the area of arts and crafts. The name of the establishment alludes to the royal support received. In 1900/01 Hirschwald managed to merge his studio with that of Henry van de Velde for a short while. Ernst Friedmann (1876–unknown) and Hermann Weber (1876–1937) took over the house in 1906, both having worked previously at Keller & Reiner and produced decorative furnishings and interior decor under the *Friedmann & Weber* name.

In dem Neubau **Königgrätzer Straße 8**, von dem Architekten Hermann Dernburg (1868–1935) errichtet, eröffneten Ernst Friedmann und Hermann Weber 1913 ein Kaufhaus großen Stils, in dessen perfekt komponierten Schauräumen allgemeine Stilfragen behandelt, aber gleichzeitig kleinste Luxus- und Gebrauchsgegenstände dargeboten wurden.

In the brand-new building **Königgrätzer Straße 8**, constructed by architect Hermann Dernburg (1868–1935), Ernst Friedmann and Hermann Weber opened a grand department store in 1913, in whose exquisitely composed showrooms staff dispensed advice on general matters of style and also presented small luxury and second-hand items for sale.

24 Potsdamer Platz

Luftaufnahme des **Potsdamer Platzes**, rechts der Leipziger Platz, von da aus im Uhrzeigersinn abgehend die Königgrätzer Straße, die Potsdamer Straße, die Bellevuestraße und die sich fortsetzende Königgrätzer Straße, 1919.

Aerial view of **Potsdamer Platz** with Leipziger Platz to the right. Clockwise meeting there are Königgrätzer Straße, Potsdamer Straße, Bellevuestraße and the continuing Königgrätzer Straße, 1919.

Der **Potsdamer Platz** mit Blick in die Bellevuestraße (links) und die Königgrätzer Straße (rechts), an der Ecke das Grand Hotel Bellevue, 1903.

Potsdamer Platz, with a view into Bellevuestraße (left) and Königgrätzer Straße (right), 1903. On the corner, the Grand Hotel Bellevue.

25 Bellevuestraße 3
Verein Berliner Künstler

Carl Meinhard, Tilla Durieux und Rudolf Bernauer während ihres Kabaretts *Kinderball der bösen Buben* im Vereinshaus in der Bellevuestraße, 1904.

Carl Meinhard, Tilla Durieux and Rudolf Bernauer during their cabaret *Children's Bad Boys Ball* on Society premises in Bellevuestraße, 1904.

Der **Verein Berliner Künstler** wurde 1841 von Künstlern und Architekten gegründet. In dem Vereinshaus gab es Platz für einen regelmäßigen Austausch der Künstler und für unterschiedliche Veranstaltungen, der Verein organisierte auch Hilfskassen für notleidende Künstler und deren Familien. Zu seinen Aufgaben zählten außerdem die Ausrichtung von Ausstellungen innerhalb seines Hauses sowie außerhalb, wie die seit 1893 jährlich stattfindende Große Berliner Kunstausstellung. Als ein besonderer Höhepunkt des Vereinslebens fand darüber hinaus ein jährliches Künstlerfest, gern als Kostümfest gestaltet, statt.

The **Society of Berlin Artists** was set up by a group of artists and architects in 1841. Their premises had room for regular meetings of artists and a range of events, with the Society also collecting money for impecunious artists and their families. It also hosted exhibitions on and off the premises, one of which was the annual Grand Berlin Art Exhibition established in 1893. One highpoint in their calendar was the annual art fair, which was also conceived as a costume festival.

Bellevuestraße 3. Das Gebäude hatte der Verein Berlin Künstler als Künstlerhaus von dem Architekten Karl Hoffacker errichten lassen und 1898 bezogen. Neben Ausstellungs- und Geschäftsräumen befanden sich hier ein großer Festsaal mit Bühne, Gesellschaftsräume, eine Bibliothek, eine Kostüm- und Waffenkammer und ein Billardzimmer. Aufgrund wirtschaftlicher Schwierigkeiten musste das Haus 1928 verkauft und 1931/32 endgültig aufgegeben werden.

Bellevuestraße 3. The Berlin Künstler Society contracted architect Karl Hoffacker to erect a building to serve as studio space for artists. The establishment featured not only exhibition rooms and meeting rooms but also a spacious functions hall and stage, a library, a costumes and weapons depository and a billiards room. After moving in in 1898, the Society was forced to sell the building in 1928 due to financial difficulties, finally vacating the premises in 1931/32.

26 Bellevuestraße 5
Cornelie Richter

Cornelie Richter (1842–1922), Tochter Giacomo Meyerbeers, hier mit ihrem Mann, dem Maler Gustav Richter (1823–84), mit dem sie seit den 1870er-Jahren gemeinsam Zusammenkünfte von Künstlern mit aufwendigen Programmpunkten wie Atelierfesten und Konzerten initiierte. Ab 1890 öffnete sie ihr Haus täglich für einen Salon, in dem sich zahlreiche prominente Kulturschaffende wie Wilhelm von Bode, Ernst Dohm, Ernst von Ihne, Harry Graf Kessler, Adolph von Menzel, Max Reinhardt, Hugo von Tschudi oder Henry van de Velde regelmäßig trafen.[5]

From the 1870s onwards **Cornelie Richter** (1842–1922), daughter of Giacomo Meyerbeer, here with her husband, painter Gustav Richter (1823–84), with whom she went to considerable effort and expense organising studio parties and concerts as a way of bringing artists together. From 1890 on they hosted a daily salon frequented by well-known cultural figures such as Wilhelm von Bode, Ernst Dohm, Ernst von Ihne, Harry Graf Kessler, Adolph von Menzel, Max Reinhardt, Hugo von Tschudi and Henry van de Velde.[5]

Blick vom Potsdamer Platz in die **Bellevuestraße**, um 1905, zu sehen sind die Hausnummern 2 (im Vordergrund), daneben in der Nr. 3 das Haus des Vereins Berliner Künstler, zwei Häuser weiter die Nr. 5. Das Haus Bellevuestraße 5 wurde 1826 als zweigeschossiges Wohnhaus mit Seitenflügel errichtet. Ab 1866 ist im Berliner Adressbuch als Eigentümerin Minna Meyerbeer, die Witwe Giacomo Meyerbeers, verzeichnet. Minna Meyerbeer selbst wohnte am Pariser Platz, in der Bellevuestraße lebte das Ehepaar Richter. 1867/68 entstand vermutlich im Auftrag von Minna Meyerbeer der Anbau eines zweigeschossigen Gartensaales an der Hinterfront, ausgeführt von den Architekten Hermann von der Hude und Julius Hennicke.

View from Potsdamer Platz into **Bellevuestraße**, ca. 1905, with numbers 2 (in the foreground) and number 3 next to it, home of the Berlin Künstler Society. Further down is Bellevuestraße 5, which was erected as a two-storey residence with side wing. From 1866 onwards the house was listed as belonging to Minna Meyerbeer, widow of Giacomo Meyerbeer. Minna Meyerbeer herself lived at Pariser Platz, while a Mr and Mrs Richter occupied the Bellevue property. In 1867/68, doubtless on the instructions of Minna Meyerbeer, a two-storey garden-hall extension was added at the rear, a project realised by architects Hermann von der Hude and Julius Hennicke.

27 Bellevuestraße 10
Lucian Bernhard

Das Speisezimmer in der Wohnung Lucian Bernhard, vor 1919.

The dining room in Lucian Bernhard's flat, before 1919.

Lucian Bernhard, eigentlich Emil Kahn (1883–1972), Grafiker, Designer und Architekt, wurde unter anderem durch seine Plakatentwürfe für Firmen wie Bosch, Pelikan, die Zigarettenfabrik Manoli und das Schuhhaus Stiller berühmt. Im Jahr 1923 erhielt er an der Unterrichtsanstalt des Berliner Kunstgewerbemuseums die erste Professur für Plakatkunst.

Lucian Bernhard, a.k.a. Emil Kahn (1883–1972), graphic artist, designer and architect, made his name with, among other achievements, his posters designed for companies such as Bosch, Pelikan, the Manoli cigarette factory and the shoe firm, Stiller. In 1923 he took up the first professorship in poster design at the educational department of the Berlin Kunstgewerbemuseum.

Bellevuestraße 10. Der Kemperplatz mit dem Rolandbrunnen, links die Lennéstraße, rechts die Bellevuestraße, 1904. In dem Eckhaus wohnte und arbeitete Lucian Bernhard in den Jahren 1911/12 bis 1918. Außerdem befanden sich hier von 1908 bis 1917 im Erdgeschoss die Deutschen Werkstätten für angewandte Handwerkskunst, ein Zusammenschluss der Münchner Vereinigten Werkstätten und der Dresdner Werkstätten für Handwerkskunst, für die Lucian Bernhard als Entwerfer tätig war.

Bellevuestraße 10. Kemperplatz with the Roland fountain, 1904; left: Lennéstraße, right: Bellevustraße. Lucian Bernhard lived and worked in the house on the corner from 1911/12 to 1918. The ground floor of the building housed the German Workshops for Applied Handicrafts between 1908 and 1917. Lucian Bernhard worked as a designer for this umbrella organisation representing the United Munich Workshops and the Dresden Workshops for Handicrafts.

28 Bellevuestraße 16–18
Hotel Esplanade

Hotel Esplanade, Blick in den Wintergarten, 1908.

Hotel Esplanade, view into the conservatory, 1908.

Bellevuestraße 16–18. Das Hotel Esplanade wurde 1907/08 im Auftrag einer Bauträgergesellschaft durch den Architekten Otto Rehnig als Grand Hôtel errichtet. Zu der prachtvollen Ausstattung gehörte unter anderem ein Festsaal, der an einen feudalen Spiegelsaal des Rokoko erinnerte. Gleichzeitig setzte das Hotel neue technische und sanitäre Standards. Als eine der ersten Adressen Berlins war es zunächst für adelige Besucher reserviert – im sogenannten Kaisersaal hielt zum Beispiel Kaiser Wilhelm II. Herrenabende ab. Mit dem Ende des Ersten Weltkriegs öffnete sich das Haus, in den 1920er-Jahren übernachteten hier Charlie Chaplin oder Greta Garbo. Heute sind der Kaiser- und der Frühstückssaal in das Sony Center am Potsdamer Platz integriert.

Bellevuestraße 16–18. The Hotel Esplanade was commissioned by a property-development company and built as a luxury hotel to plans by the architect Otto Rehnig. The opulent interior included a ballroom reminiscent of a rococo-style hall of mirrors, yet the establishment also set new technical and sanitary standards. As one of Berlin's finest addresses, it was initially reserved for the aristocracy; Emperor Wilhelm II hosted gentlemen's evenings in the "Kaisersaal", for example. At the end of the First World War the hotel was opened up to a wider clientele, with Charlie Chaplin and Greta Garbo staying here in the 1920s. The "Kaisersaal" and breakfast hall are today part of the Sony Center at Potsdamer Platz.

29   Kemperplatz

Kemperplatz mit Blick in die Bellevuestraße, 2015.

Kemperplatz with view into Bellevuestraße, 2015.

Der **Kemperplatz** mit dem Rolandbrunnen, mit Blick in die Bellevuestraße, links die Lennéstraße, um 1926.

Kemperplatz with the Roland fountain. View into Bellevuestraße; left: Lennéstraße, ca. 1926.

30 Siegesallee

Siegesallee, Gruppe Nr. 33: Friedrich III. (1831–88), gestaltet von dem Bildhauer Adolf Brütt. Die Büste links stellt den Generalfeldmarschall Leonhard von Blumenthal (1810–1900) dar, der Friedrich III. bei mehreren Feldzügen zur Seite stand, rechts ist der Physiker und liberale Politiker Hermann von Helmholtz (1821–94) zu sehen, der an die Fortschrittsbegeisterung Friedrichs III., aber auch an dessen viel diskutierte liberale Gesinnung erinnert.

Siegesallee, Group no. 33: Friedrich III (1831–88), designed by sculptor Adolf Brütt. The bust on the left depicts Field Marshal Leonhard von Blumenthal (1810–1900), a stalwart of several military campaigns. On the left is the physicist and liberal politician Hermann von Helmholtz (1821–94), a reference to Friedrich III's enthusiasm for progress and much-vaunted liberal outlook.

Siegesallee. Kaiser Wilhelm II. (1849–1941) ließ die rund 750 Meter lange, im Tiergarten vom Kemperplatz zum Königsplatz (heute Platz der Republik) verlaufende Allee bis 1901 als eine Art Ahnengalerie erweitern. In der Siegesallee standen mehr als 30 Gruppen mit Marmordenkmälern, die von 27 unterschiedlichen Bildhauern geschaffen wurden. Gerahmt wurden die Markgrafen und Kurfürsten von Brandenburg sowie die preußischen Könige und Kaiser von je zwei Büsten nahestehender Personen.

Siegesallee. Kaiser Wilhelm II (1849–1941) had the 750-metre-long boulevard running through the Tiergarten from Kemperplatz to Königsplatz (today's Platz der Republik) extended to create a kind of ancestral throroughfare. Completed in 1901 and the work of 27 sculptors, the Siegesallee featured more than 30 groups of figures with marble monuments. Flanked were the margrave or elector of Brandenburg or one of the Prussian kings and emperors by two busts depicting associated dignitaries.

31 In den Zelten 23
Felicie Bernstein

Felicie Bernstein (ca. 1852–1908) führte zunächst in der Lennéstraße und später unter der Adresse In den Zelten einen Salon. Zu ihren Gästen zählten viele leitende Museumsmitarbeiter, so Wilhelm von Bode, Ernst Curtius, Friedrich Lippmann, Hugo von Tschudi und Werner Weisbach, aber auch zahlreiche Maler wie Curt Herrmann, Max Klinger, Walter Leistikow, Reinhold Lepsius, Max Liebermann und Adolph von Menzel.[6] Außerdem waren Felicie und ihr Ehemann Carl Bernstein (1842–94) leidenschaftliche Kunstsammler und besaßen die ersten Bilder französischer Impressionisten in Berlin.

Felicie Bernstein (ca. 1852–1908) hosted a salon, first on Lennéstraße, then on the In den Zelten thoroughfare. Her guests included many leading members of various museum staffs, such as Wilhelm von Bode, Ernst Curtius, Friedrich Lippmann, Hugo von Tschudi and Werner Weisbach, and also painters of the likes of Curt Herrmann, Max Klinger, Walter Leistikow, Reinhold Lepsius, Max Liebermann and Adolph von Menzel.[6] Felicie and her husband Carl Bernstein (1842–94) were keen art collectors and the owners of the first French Impressionist paintings to come to Berlin.

In den Zelten 23. Einen Einblick in die Sammlung und Ausstattung der bis 1891 genutzten Wohnung von Felicie und Carl Bernstein gibt diese 1914 publizierte Aufnahme ihres Musikzimmers. Zu sehen sind neben französischen Möbeln des 18. Jahrhunderts zeitgenössische Gemälde, unter anderem von Édouard Manet, Camille Pissarro und Alfred Sisley.

In den Zelten 23. This view of the music room, dated 1914, affords a glimpse of the art and furnishings in the flat occupied by Felicie and Carl Bernstein until 1891. The photograph shows 18th-century French furniture and contemporary paintings by masters such as Édouard Manet, Camille Pissarro and Alfred Sisley.

32 Tiergartenstraße 4
Valentin Weisbach

Valentin Weisbach (1843–1899), Bankier und Börsenmakler, sammelte zunächst Grafik und wurde dabei von dem Direktor des Kupferstichkabinetts Friedrich Lippmann unterstützt, dann vor allem alte Kunst, wobei er sich auf das Urteil Wilhelm von Bodes sowie auf Julius Lessing, den Direktor des Berliner Kunstgewerbemuseums, verließ.[7] Valentin Weisbach unterstütze die Museen sowohl finanziell als auch durch Schenkungen und gehörte zu den Gründungsmitgliedern des Kaiser-Friedrich-Museums-Vereins. Außerdem engagierte er sich im sozialen Wohnungsbau.

Valentin Weisbach (1843–1899), banker and stockbroker, initially collected graphic art and was supported in this by the director of the Kupferstichkabinett, Friedrich Lippmann. Weisbach then switched his attentions to ancient artworks, relying on the judgement of Wilhelm von Bode and Julius Lessing, director of the Berlin Kunstgewerbemuseum.[7] He supported the work of the Berlin museums by donating money and artworks and was one of the founding members of the Kaiser Friedrich Museum Society. He was also involved in the construction of social housing.

Tiergartenstraße 4. Valentin Weisbach ist für das Grundstück, auf welchem seit 1826 ein eingeschossiges Wohnhaus stand, seit 1876 als Eigentümer eingetragen. 1888 ließ Weisbach das Haus abreißen und von dem Architekten Christian Heidecke eine Villa errichten, die bis 1909 im Besitz seiner Erben blieb. Dann erwarb sie der Fabrikant Georg Liebermann (1844–1926). Liebermanns Erben vermieteten sie unter anderem an die Auktionatoren Paul Graupe und Hermann Ball, 1940 wurde die Familie Liebermann enteignet. Die Nationalsozialisten nutzten die Villa danach für die Verwaltung der sogenannten „Aktion T4", mit der die systematische Ermordung von Psychiatriepatienten und Behinderten organisiert wurde.

Tiergartenstraße 4. From 1876 onwards Valentin Weisbach was listed as the owner of the property, which featured a single-storey residence. In 1888 Weisbach demolished the building and had architect Christian Heidecke erect a villa in its place, which remained in the Weisbach family until 1909, when it was bought by factory owner Georg Liebermann (1844–1926). Liebermann's heirs rented the villa out. Tenants included Paul Graupe (see next pages) and Hermann Ball. The Liebermanns were expropriated in 1940. The National Socialists used the villa as their coordination centre for "Aktion T4", the systematic murder of psychiatric patients and disabled people.

32 Tiergartenstraße 4
Paul Graupe

Paul Graupe (1881–1953), Kunsthändler und Auktionator, begann 1916 mit Versteigerungen von Büchersammlungen, später nahm er auch Grafiken, Gemälde und Antiquitäten hinzu, für die er innerhalb von knapp 20 Jahren erfolgreich rund 160 Auktionen veranstaltete. 1927 schloss sich Graupe mit dem Auktionator Hermann Ball zusammen, beide hatten in den Jahren 1928 bis 1931 ihren Sitz in der Tiergartenstraße 4.

Paul Graupe (1881–1953), art dealer and auctioneer, began selling book collections to the highest bidder in 1916. He extended his activity to drawings, paintings and antiques, holding approximately 160 successful auctions over a 20-year-period. In 1927 Graupe merged his operations with auctioneer Hermann Ball. Both maintained offices at the Tiergartenstraße 4 address between 1928 and 1931.

Tiergartenstraße 4. Die Bibliothek in den Geschäftsräumen von Paul Graupe wurde von dem Architekten Paul Huldschinsky eingerichtet, der in der Regentenstraße 20 wohnte.

Tiergartenstraße 4. The Library in Paul Graupe's office was installed by architect Paul Huldschinsky, who lived at Regentenstraße 20.

33 Tiergartenstraße 8a
Benoit Oppenheim

Benoit Oppenheim (1842–um 1931), Bankier, sammelte mittelalterliche Kunst aus Deutschland, Flandern und Frankreich, vor allem Skulpturen, mit denen er sich auch wissenschaftlich auseinandersetzte.[8] Außerdem erwarb Oppenheim nach Beratung durch Wilhelm von Bode zahlreiche Kunstwerke, so eine große Anzahl antiker Möbel aus Frankreich, die er in seine neu errichtete Villa in der Tiergartenstraße integrierte, wie hier in seinem Billardzimmer. Zuvor hatte Benoit Oppenheim bis 1897 ein Haus in der Bellevuestraße 3 besessen und bewohnt, das er später dem Verein Berliner Künstler verkaufte, der auf diesem Grundstück sein neues Vereinshaus errichtete.

Benoit Oppenheim (1842–ca. 1931), banker, collected mediaeval art stemming from Germany, Flanders and France and focused his attentions on sculpture, in which he also took a scientific interest.[8] Assisted by Wilhelm von Bode, Oppenheim also amassed many other works of art including numerous pieces of French furniture, with which he furnished his newly built villa on Tiergartenstraße, for example his billiards room. Up until 1897 Benoit Oppenheim was owner-occupier of the house at Bellevuestraße 3, which he sold to the Society of Berlin Artists, who proceeded to erect a new clubhouse on the plot of land.

Tiergartenstraße 8a. Benoit Oppenheim ließ die hier stehende Villa 1896/97 von dem Architekten Christian Heidecke erbauen.

Tiergartenstraße 8a. Benoit Oppenheim built this villa in 1896/97 to plans by the architect Christian Heidecke.

34 Tiergartenstraße 14
Marcus Kappel

Marcus Kappel (1839–1919), Bankier und Kaufmann, besaß eine große Kunstsammlung mit einem Schwerpunkt auf der holländischen Malerei des 17. Jahrhunderts mit Werken von Rembrandt, Rubens, van Dyck und Frans Hals, die auf Anraten Wilhelm von Bodes entstand. Gleichzeitig erweitere er seine Sammlung durch zeitgenössische Arbeiten, so mehrere von Adolph von Menzel. Für die Präsentation dieser Werke hatte er in seinem Wohnhaus einen eigenen Galerieraum mit Oberlicht eingerichtet (siehe Abbildung rechte Seite).

Marcus Kappel (1839–1919), banker and merchant, built up a large art collection dominated by Dutch paintings of the 17th century, including works by Rembrandt, Rubens, van Dyck and Frans Hals. He, too, benefited from the advice of Wilhelm von Bode. At the same time his collection was growing as a result of his acquisition of paintings by contemporary artists such as Adolph von Menzel. To display these masterpieces Kappel had a gallery with skylight installed in his residence, which is shown on the right.

Tiergartenstraße 14. Das Haus wurde 1868/69 als Wohnhaus im Auftrag von Odilon de Craecker, Königlich Belgischer Generalkonsul, von dem Architekten F. A. W. Strauch errichtet. Laut den Einträgen im Berliner Adressbuch war ab 1881 Marcus Kappel Eigentümer des Hauses, er blieb aber bis 1882 als Bewohner in der Regentenstraße 16 gemeldet.

Tiergartenstraße 14. The residence was commissioned in 1868/69 by Odilon de Craecker, the Royal Belgian Consul, and constructed by F. A. W. Strauch. Entries in the Berlin address book list Marcus Kappel as the proprietor from 1881 onwards, although Kappel himself was registered as living at Regentenstraße 16 until 1882.

35 Tiergartenstraße 15 a
James Simon

James Simon (1851–1932) leitete die Baumwoll- und Leinenfabrik Gebr. Simon und war Vetter von Eduard Simon.⁹ 1911 stand er an sechster Stelle der Berliner Einkommensliste. Früh baute er mit Hilfe Wilhelm von Bodes eine Kunstsammlung auf, 1885 besaß er seinen ersten Rembrandt. Simon gehörte zu den größten Mäzenen der Berliner Museen. Zur Eröffnung des Kaiser-Friedrich-Museums stiftete er seine umfangreiche Renaissancesammlung, die unter anderem das Bild *Maria mit dem schlafenden Kind* von Andrea Mantegna enthielt. Simon half auch, die Ausgrabungen des Deutschen Reiches im Vorderen Orient zu realisieren. 1913 schenkte er den Berliner Museen alle Funde, darunter die Büste der Nofretete. Außerdem engagierte er sich sozial und spendete jährlich eine Summe von umgerechnet mehreren Millionen Euro.

James Simon (1851–1932) was a cousin of Eduard Simon and a partner in, and later the manager of, the very successful cotton and linen factory, Gebr. Simon.⁹ In 1911 he was ranked sixth on the list of high-earning Berliners. His trajectory as a collector began early, with Simon accumulating ancient art helped by tips from Wilhelm von Bode. By 1885 he already owned his first Rembrandt. Simon was one of the great patrons of the arts linked to the Berlin Museums. To mark the inauguration of the Kaiser Friedrich Museum he donated his entire collection of Renaissance art, which included *Madonna with Sleeping Child* by Andrea Mantegna. Simon was a generous funder of excavations undertaken by the German Empire in the Middle East. In 1913 he donated all his finds, including the bust of Nefertiti, to the Berlin Museums. James Simon also showed commitment to the idea of social justice, making annual donations (several million euros in today's money).

Tiergartenstraße 15a. James Simon wohnte mit seiner Frau Agnes und den drei Kindern in der 1885/86 von dem Architekten Carl Schwatlo (1831–84) errichteten Villa. 1909 gab Simon einen Umbau durch Alfred Breslauer (1866–1954) in Auftrag, der vor allem dazu diente, seine umfangreiche Sammlung im Erdgeschoss zu präsentieren. Diese war nach Voranmeldung auch Besuchern zugänglich.

Tiergartenstraße 15a. James Simon lived with his wife Agnes and their three children in this villa built by architect Carl Schwatlo (1831–84). In 1909 Simon commissioned Alfred Breslauer (1866–1954) to modify the premises. The changes were designed primarily in order to make way on the ground floor for his extensive collection. Visitors could also view the collection by appointment.

36 Regentenstraße 19
Eduard Arnhold

Eduard Arnhold (1849–1925), Kaufmann, Inhaber eines Kohlengroßhandels, sammelte zunächst deutsche zeitgenössische Malerei, hinzu kam durch den Einfluss Wilhelm von Bodes auch alte Kunst.[10] Ab Ende des 19. Jahrhunderts erwarb Arnhold zusätzlich moderne französische Gemälde von Manet, Sisley, Pissarro, Degas, Renoir, aber auch von van Gogh bei der Kunsthandlung Cassirer. Seine Sammlung, die er im eigens dafür entworfenen Galerieraum präsentierte, umfasste insgesamt mehr als 250 Gemälde, knapp 70 moderne Skulpturen und etliche Kleinplastiken von der Frührenaissance bis zum 18. Jahrhundert.

Eduard Arnhold (1849–1925), a merchant and coal wholesaler, initially collected German paintings of the day, moving on to ancient art under the influence of Wilhelm von Bode.[10] From the late 19th century Arnhold bought modern French works by Manet, Sisley, Pissarro, Degas and Renoir and also by van Gogh from Cassirer's art dealership. His collection, which he put on display in a gallery designed specially to accommodate it, ran to over 250 paintings, nigh on 70 pieces of modern sculpture and numerous smaller sculptures stretching from the Early Renaissance to the 18th century.

Regentenstraße 19. Das Gebäude wurde 1898 von Eduard Arnhold gekauft und umgehend von den Architekten Heinrich Kayser und Karl von Großheim, die es drei Jahre zuvor errichtet hatten, durch einen Oberlichtsaal ergänzt, der 1912 von dem Architekten Paul Baumgarten auf letztendlich 200 Quadratmeter erweitert wurde, um Teile der Kunstsammlung Arnholds zu präsentieren.

Regentenstraße 19. Purchased by Eduard Arnhold in 1898, the building had a sky-lit hall added by architects Heinrich Kayser and Karl von Großheim, who had designed the house three years earlier. This hall was in turn enlarged in 1912 by Paul Baumgarten to cover 200 square metres and accommodate a portion of Arnhold's art collection.

37 Regentenstraße 20
Paul Huldschinsky

Paul Huldschinsky (1889–1947), Illustrator und Innenarchitekt, arbeitete zunächst in München und dann in Berlin, wo er mehrere Häuser insbesondere im Tiergartenviertel einrichtete, so zum Beispiel die Geschäftsräume von Paul Graupe in der Tiergartenstraße 4. 1939 emigrierte er nach einer mehrmonatigen Haft im Konzentrationslager Sachsenhausen in die USA, wo er als Ausstatter beim Film bekannt wurde.

Paul Huldschinsky (1889–1947), illustrator and interior designer, worked first in Munich, then in Berlin, where he furnished a number of houses in the Tiergarten district, properties that included the offices of Paul Graupe at Tiergartenstraße 4. In 1939, after several months of internment in Sachsenhausen concentration camp, he emigrated to the USA, where he worked as a set designer in the film industry.

Regentenstraße 20. Das Haus wurde 1862/63 von dem Architekten Carl Busse als Mietshaus errichtet. Nach seiner Rückkehr aus München war Paul Huldschinsky 1928 im Berliner Adressbuch bei seinem Vater in der Matthäikirchstraße 3a gemeldet, ab 1929 in der Regentenstraße 20.

Regentenstraße 20. This house was built in 1862/63 by Carl Busse as a rental property. On his return from Munich in 1928 Paul Huldschinsky moved in with his father at Matthäikirchstraße 3a, according to the Berlin address book. From 1929 onwards he was listed as resident at Regentenstraße 20.

38 Regentenstraße 24
Georg Kolbe

Georg Kolbe (1877–1947), Bildhauer, schuf zeitlebens Aktfiguren und Büsten vor allem aus Bronze. Berühmt wurde er mit seiner Plastik *Die Tänzerin* von 1911/12, die 1912 auf der Frühjahrsausstellung der Berliner Secession ausgestellt und wenig später von der Berliner Nationalgalerie angekauft wurde. Von ihm stammen zahlreiche öffentliche Denkmäler in Deutschland. Georg Kolbe war eng mit Paul Cassirer befreundet, der zugleich sein wichtigster Kunsthändler war und ihm 1921 eine große Einzelausstellung in seiner Galerie in der Victoriastraße widmete.

Georg Kolbe (1877–1947), sculptor, worked mostly in bronze, producing assorted nudes and busts. His breakthrough came with *The Dancer* (1911/12), which was included in the exhibition of Berlin Secession paintings in the spring of 1912 and shortly afterwards bought by the Berlin Nationalgalerie. Kolbe created numerous public monuments throughout Germany. He was a close friend of Paul Cassirer, who was his biggest art dealer and organised a major solo exhibition of his works in the Victoriastraße gallery in 1921.

Regentenstraße 24. Das Gebäude wurde gemeinsam mit der Nr. 23 in den Jahren 1863–65 von dem Architekten Carl Ferdinand Busse und dessen Sohn Carl Busse als Doppelmietshaus errichtet. Georg Kolbe hatte hier in den 1920er-Jahren sein Atelier eingerichtet, er wohnte in dieser Zeit in der nahegelegenen Von-der-Heydt-Straße.

Regentenstraße 24. This building and its neighbour, No. 23, were designed in 1863–65 as a rental property by architects Carl Ferdinand Busse and his son Carl Busse. Georg Kolbe worked here in the 1920s and resided close by in Von-der-Heydt-Straße.

39 Bendlerstraße 9/Königin-Augusta-Straße 19
Max Liebermann

Max Liebermann (1847–1935), Maler und Grafiker, ab 1897 Professor an der Königlichen Akademie der Künste. Sein erstes öffentlich ausgestelltes Werk, die 1872 auf der Berliner Akademieausstellung gezeigten *Gänserupferinnen*, bescherte ihm viel Kritik, aber auch große Aufmerksamkeit – ein Gegensatz, der ihn während der nächsten Jahre begleiten sollte. 1898 gehörte er zu den Gründern der Berliner Secession, deren erster Präsident er wurde. 1892 bezog Max Liebermann das Palais seiner Familie am Pariser Platz als Wohn- und Atelierhaus und ab 1910 zusätzlich sein von Paul Baumgarten errichtetes Landhaus am Wannsee.

Max Liebermann (1847–1935), painter and graphic artist, from 1897 Professor of the Royal Academy of Arts. His first publicly shown work, *Women Plucking Geese*, attracted criticism for its naturalistic style but also much attention – a contradictory form of reception that he was to experience often in the years to come. In 1898 he was one of the founders of the Berlin Secession and became its first president. Aside from his primary residence on Pariser Platz, Max Liebermann commissioned the architect Paul Baumgarten in 1909/10 to build him a country house on the shores of the Großer Wannsee.

Bendlerstraße 9/Königin-Augusta-Straße 19.
Anschließend an längere Auslandsaufenthalte lebte Max Liebermann nach seiner Heirat 1884 laut Berliner Adressbuch zunächst im Tiergartenviertel im Haus In den Zelten 11 und von 1889 bis 1892 in der Bendlerstraße 9, einem Gebäude, das seinem Vetter Emil Rathenau gehörte. Im Nachbarhaus, der Bendlerstraße 10, wohnte der Historiker Felix Liebermann, ein jüngerer Bruder von Max, zu dem er ein enges Verhältnis hatte. Das Atelier Liebermanns befand sich in dieser Zeit in der Königin-Augusta-Straße 19.

Bendlerstraße 9/Königin-Augusta-Straße 19.
After his marriage in 1884, and when he was not spending extended periods abroad, Max Liebermann resided firstly at In den Zelten 11 in the Tiergarten district and between 1889 and 1892 at Bendlerstraße 9 in a house belonging to his cousin Emil Rathenau. The historian Felix Liebermann, a younger brother with whom Max had a particularly close relationship, lived next door at No. 10. During this period Liebermann's studio was located at Königin-Augusta-Straße 19.

Max Liebermann in seinem Atelier in der Königin-Augusta-Straße 19, o.J.

Max Liebermann in his studio in Königin-Augusta-Straße 19, undated.

40 Genthiner Straße 13 i
Julius Meier-Graefe, Luise Begas-von Parmentier

Julius Meier-Graefe (1867–1935), Kunsthistoriker und Schriftsteller. In zahlreichen Publikationen widmete er sich der modernen, vor allem französischen Malerei. Außerdem war er Mitbegründer der Zeitschriften *Pan* und *Dekorative Kunst* und eröffnete in Paris, wo er ab 1896 zumeist lebte, die Maison Moderne, eine bis 1903 bestehende Galerie für modernes Kunstgewerbe. Veröffentlichungen wie sein erster Band über die Entwicklungsgeschichte der modernen Kunst (1904) und *Der Fall Böcklin und die Lehre von den Einheiten* (1905) brachten ihm Kritik und den Vorwurf ein, die „deutsche Kunst" in ein schlechtes Licht zu stellen. Während seiner Berlinaufenthalte wohnte Meier-Graefe in der Genthiner Straße 13 i, im Berliner Adressbuch ist er hier für die Jahre 1900, 1907–09 und 1910/11 verzeichnet.

Julius Meier-Graefe (1867–1935), art historian and writer. Many of his published texts explored modern art, in particular French painting. He was co-founder of two journals, *Pan* and *Dekorative Kunst*, and in Paris, where he spent most of his time from 1896 onwards, he opened the Maison Moderne, a gallery for modern decorative arts that survived until 1903. Publications such as his first volume on the development of modern art (1904) and *Der Fall Böcklin und die Lehre von den Einheiten* (1905) earned him bad notices and the charge that he showed "German art" in a bad light. When in Berlin Meier-Graefe would stay at Genthiner Straße 13 i. The Berlin address book lists this as his residence in 1900, 1907–09 and 1910/11.

Luise Begas-von Parmentier (1850–1920), Malerin, stellvertretende Vorsitzende des Vereins der Künstlerinnen. Luise Begas-von Parmentier war verheiratet mit dem Maler Adalbert Begas (1835–88); sie wurde früh Witwe und vermietete Zimmer in ihrem Haus in der Genthiner Straße. Seit den 1880er-Jahren führte sie einen Salon mit Gästen aus der Kunstwelt, Musik und Literatur in ihrem Haus in der Genthiner Straße 13i. Zu der Wohngruppe unter der Adresse 13, auch als „Begaswinkel" bekannt, gehörten ursprünglich acht Häuser. Sie wurde 1871 von dem Architekten Ernst Klingenberg im Auftrag wohlhabender Bürger errichtet. Das Wohnhaus von Luise Begas-von Parmentier ist noch erhalten und hat heute die Adresse Genthiner Straße 30i.

Luise Begas-von Parmentier (1850–1920), painter and Deputy Chairperson of the Society of Female Artists. Luise Begas-von Parmentier was married to painter Adalbert Begas (1835–88); widowed early, she rented out rooms in her home on Genthiner Straße. From the 1880s onwards she hosted a salon attracting guests from the world of art, music and letters in her villa on Genthiner Straße 13i. Eight houses used to form the ensemble at No. 13, also known as "Begas Nook". Contracted by wealthy citizens, the architect Ernst Klingenberg built the complex in 1871. The residence belonging to Luise Begas-von Parmentier – Genthiner Straße 30i – survives to this day.

41 Genthiner Straße 43
Max Jacob Friedländer

Der Restaurator Aloys Hauser, Max Friedländer und Wilhelm von Bode (v.l.n.r.) in der Gemäldegalerie des Alten Museums, um 1920.

Restorer Aloys Hauser, Max Friedländer and Wilhelm von Bode (l. to r.) in the Gemäldegalerie of the Altes Museum, ca. 1920.

Max Jacob Friedländer (1867–1958), Kunsthistoriker, von 1896 bis 1933 an der Berliner Gemäldegalerie beschäftigt, ab 1924 deren Direktor, leitete außerdem zwischen 1908 und 1930 das Kupferstichkabinett. Friedländer spezialisierte sich auf die altniederländische und altdeutsche Kunst, er publizierte mehr als 800 Werke, war ein gefragter Gutachter und verhalf den Berliner Museen zu herausragenden Erwerbungen. 1939 emigrierte Max Friedländer in die Niederlande.

Max Jacob Friedländer (1867–1958), art historian, on the staff of the Gemäldegalerie from 1896 to 1933 (Director from 1924 onwards) and Director of the Kupferstichkabinett between 1908 and 1930. Friedländer specialised in medieval Dutch and German art, published over 800 works, was a sought-after expert and helped the Berlin Museums make important acquisitions. In 1939 Max Friedländer emigrated to the Netherlands.

Genthiner Straße 43. Unter dieser Adresse war Max Friedländer von 1906 bis 1935 gemeldet.

Genthiner Straße 43. The registered residential address of Max Friedländer between 1906 and 1935.

42 Lützowufer 13
Alfred Flechtheim

Alfred Flechtheim (1878–1937), Kunsthändler und Sammler, Publizist und Verleger. Flechtheim begann bereits um das Jahr 1900 zeitgenössische Kunst zu sammeln, darunter Arbeiten von Pablo Picasso, Vincent van Gogh und französischer Avantgardekünstler. 1913 eröffnete er in Düsseldorf seine erste Galerie mit einer Dependance unter anderem in Berlin, wohin er 1921 seinen Hauptsitz verlegte. Auch hier zeigte und förderte er die Vertreter der europäischen Avantgarde in zahlreichen Ausstellungen, aber ebenso mithilfe gut inszenierter Eröffnungen und Abendveranstaltungen.

Alfred Flechtheim (1878–1937), art dealer and collector, writer and publisher. By the turn of the century Flechtheim was already collecting contemporary art, including works by Pablo Picasso, Vincent van Gogh and French artists of the avant-garde. In 1913 he opened his first gallery in Düsseldorf with branches in other cities, including Berlin, which became his centre of operations in 1921. Here, too, he displayed and backed the chief figures of the European avant-garde not only with his numerous exhibitions but also by means of well organised openings and evening events.

Otto Dix, *Der Kunsthändler Alfred Flechtheim*, Öl auf Leinwand, 1926.

Otto Dix, *Der Kunsthändler Alfred Flechtheim*, oil on canvas, 1926.

Lützowufer 13. Hier eröffnete Alfred Flechtheim im Jahr 1921 in angemieteten Räumen eine Galerie. Die Abbildung zeigt den Auftritt des italienischen Violinisten Giovanni Bagarotti, am Klavier von Leonora Speyer begleitet, der Tochter der berühmten US-amerikanischen Geigerin Leonora Speyer, im Jahr 1930.

Lützowufer 13. In 1921 Alfred Flechtheim opened a gallery in rented space on this site. The picture shows a recital by Italian violinist Giovanni Bagarotti, accompanied on the piano by Leonora Speyer, daughter of the famed American violinist Leonora Speyer, 1930.

43 Schöneberger Ufer 71
Verein der Künstlerinnen und Kunstfreundinnen Berlins

Der **Verein der Künstlerinnen und Kunstfreundinnen Berlins** (heute Verein der Berliner Künstlerinnen) wurde 1867 von annähernd 100 Frauen gegründet, um sich für die Rechte von Künstlerinnen einzusetzen, denen der Zugang zu den Akademien verwehrt war. Der Verein organisierte Ausstellungen und fungierte als Ausbildungsstätte. Legendär waren die von ihm veranstalteten Weihnachtsmessen (seit 1887) und Kostümfeste (seit 1891), wie dem hier abgebildeten Faschingsfest im Jahr 1900, deren Einnahmen in die vereinseigene Pensions- und Altersrentenkasse flossen.

The **Berlin Society of Female Artists and Female Art Patrons** (today the Berlin Society of Female Artists) was founded in 1867 by a group of almost 100 women determined to promote the rights of women artists, who were prevented from enrolling in academies. The Society organised exhibitions and served as a place of instruction. The Christmas Fairs held by the Society (from 1887) and the costume festivals (from 1891), as shown here in the year 1900, were legendary, with the money raised going into the Society's own pensions fund.

Schöneberger Ufer 71. Das Gebäude wurde 1910/11 als Vereins- und Schulhaus des Vereins der Künstlerinnen und Kunstfreundinnen Berlins von dem Architekten Heinrich Schweitzer entworfen. Der Verein befand sich hier bis 1935. Das Haus ist erhalten, die Fassade wurde teilweise rekonstruiert.

Schöneberger Ufer 71. The building was designed in 1910/11 by architect Heinrich Schweitzer as the clubhouse and school premises of the Berlin Society of Female Artists and Female Art Patrons. The Society met here until 1935. The house survives to this day, with a partially reconstructed façade.

Anmerkungen   Notes

1   Kuhrau 2005, S. 126–27, 277.

2   Wilhelmy 1989, S. 767–72.

3   Kuhrau 2005, S. 9–24.

4   Ihne 1975/76, S. 205–211.

5   Wilhelmy 1989, S. 808–13.

6   Wilhelmy 1989, S. 612–15.

7   Kuhrau 2005, S. 80, 198.

8   Kuhrau 2005, S. 144–46, 202–03.

9   Biggeleben 2006, S. 191–218.

10 Kuhrau 2005, S. 218–23.

Literatur

Bibliography

Berliner Adressbücher. Diese liegen für die Jahre 1799–1943 digitalisiert vor, bearbeitet durch das Projekt Berlin-Studien, Zentral- und Landesbibliothek Berlin.

Bianca Berding: Der Kunsthandel in Berlin für moderne angewandte Kunst von 1897 bis 1914. Dissertationsschrift Freie Universität Berlin. Berlin 2012.

Christoph Biggeleben: Das „Bollwerk des Bürgertums". Die Berliner Kaufmannschaft 1870–1920. München 2006.

Victor von Ihne: Von der Reichskanzlei zum Kaiserhof. Mein Leben. [1975/76, unveröffentlichtes Typoskript im Bundesarchiv Koblenz, kleine Erwerbungen 908] Abgedruckt in: Oliver Sander: Die Rekonstruktion des Architekten-Nachlasses von Ernst von Ihne (1848–1917). Dissertationsschrift 2001, Humboldt-Universität. Berlin 2002 [Mikrofiche-Ausgabe].

Sven Kuhrau: Der Kunstsammler im Kaiserreich. Kunst und Repräsentation in der Berliner Privatsammlerkultur. Lübeck 2005.

Kulturforum 1. Konzept zur Weiterentwicklung – Senatsbeschluss vom 26. April 2005. Dokumentation der Beschlussvorlage und erläuternde Informationen. Hg. v. der Senatsverwaltung für Stadtentwicklung. Koordination, Konzept und Texte von Hans Stimmann. Berlin 2005.

Kulturforum 2. Der Diskussionsprozess von Juni 2004 – März 2005. Eine Dokumentation der 5 Architekturgespräche und des Online-Dialoges. Hg. v. der Senatsverwaltung für Stadtentwicklung. Koordination, Konzept und Texte von Hans Stimmann. Berlin 2005.

Kulturforum 3. Der Masterplan. Vom Konzept 2004 zum Masterplan 2005 (Senatsbeschluss, 26. April 2005) und Dokumentation über die Arbeit in der Planungswerkstatt. Hg. v. der Senatsverwaltung für Stadtentwicklung. Koordination, Konzept und Texte von Hans Stimmann. Berlin 2005.

Sylvia Lais und Hans-Jürgen Mende (Hg.): Lexikon Berliner Straßennamen. Berlin 2014.

Olaf Matthes: James Simon. Mäzen im Wilhelminischen Zeitalter. Bürgerlichkeit, Wertewandel, Mäzenatentum Bd. 5. Berlin 2000.

Sibylle Nägele und Joy Markert: Die Potsdamer Straße. Geschichten, Mythen und Metamorphosen. 2. überarbeitete und erweiterte Auflage. Berlin 2006.

Platz und Monument. Die Kontroverse um das Kulturforum 1980–1992. Hg. v. Berlinische Galerie, Museumspädagogischer Dienst Berlin. Berlin 1992.

Wolfgang Schäche und Norbert Szymanski: Die Lennéstraße im Tiergartenviertel. Geschichte und Perspektive einer Berliner Adresse. Berlin 2003.

Hartwig Schmidt: Das Tiergartenviertel. Baugeschichte eines Berliner Villenviertels. Die Bauwerke und Kunstdenkmäler von Berlin, Beiheft 4. Berlin 1981.

Hans Stimmann: Zukunft des Kulturforums. Abgesang auf die Insel der Objekte. Berlin 2012.

Werner Weisbach: Und alles ist zerstoben. Erinnerungen aus der Jahrhundertwende. Wien, Leipzig, Zürich 1937.

Petra Wilhelmy: Der Berliner Salon im 19. Jahrhundert. 1780–1914. Veröffentlichungen der Historischen Kommission zu Berlin, Bd. 73. Berlin 1989.

Ulrike Wolff-Thomsen und Sven Kuhrau (Hg.): Geschmacksgeschichten. Öffentliches und privates Kunstsammeln in Deutschland 1871–1933. Kiel 2011.

Bildnachweis

© bpk: Umschlagabbildung vorne, S. 4 (Rolf Koehler), 15, 24 oben (Nationalgalerie/SMB, Karin März), 26, 27, 28 (Zander und Labisch), 30 (Franz Kullrich), 31, 32, 35, 42, 44 (Nationalgalerie/SMB, Klaus Göken), 45, 47 (Staatsbibliothek zu Berlin/SPK), 50, 52 (Rolf Koehler), 53 (Luftbild Berlin GmbH), 55, 57 (Kunstbibliothek/SMB), 58, 59, 62, 64, 65 (Staatsbibliothek zu Berlin/SPK), 66 (Nationalgalerie/SMB, Jörg P. Anders), 70 (Luftbild Berlin GmbH), 71, 73, 74, 75, 77, 79, 81, 82 (Neue Photographische Gesellschaft), 83, 85 (Kunstbibliothek/SMB, J. Egers), 95, 96, 102 (Nicola Perscheid), 103 (Max von Rüdiger), 104, 105 (Hans Franke), 106 (Gemäldegalerie/SMB), 110

© Nina Lüth, www.ninalueth.de: S. 14, 54, 80

Staatsbibliothek zu Berlin/Stiftung Preußischer Kulturbesitz: S. 22, 23 (Digitalisierte Sammlungen: http://resolver.staatsbibliothek-berlin.de/SBB-00015CED00000000), 38, 48, 84, 92

Picture Credits

Ullstein Bild: Umschlagabbildung hinten links, S. 24 unten (Ludwig Boedecker), 34 (Alice Matzdorff), 46 (Waldemar Titzenthaler), 51, 72 (Süddeutsche Zeitung Photo/Scherl), 88, 89, 94, 97 (Rudolph Duehrkoop), 98 (Ernst Sandau), 109 (Dephot)

Landesarchiv Berlin: Kartenausschnitte in den Umschlagseiten (HistoMap Berlin), S. 25, 33, 37, 39, 41, 87 (alle Walter Köster); 40, 43, 86, 107

Archiv der Autorin: S. 29, 36, 49, 56, 63, 93, 99

Kunstbibliothek/Staatliche Museen zu Berlin: S. 60, 61, 69, 101 (Scans von Dietmar Katz)

Architekturmuseum der Technischen Universität Berlin in der Universitätsbibliothek: S. 68
Zentralarchiv/Staatliche Museen zu Berlin: S. 90, 91

Christian Günther: S. 111

© VG Bild-Kunst, Bonn 2019 für Marc Chagall (S. 65), Henry van de Velde (S. 67) und Otto Dix (S. 108)

Register

Index

Arnhold, Eduard   S. 10, 29, 44, 96–97
Bagarotti, Giovanni   S. 109
Ball, Hermann   S. 87–88
Bamberger, Ludwig   S. 39
Baumgarten, Paul   S. 97, 102
Begas, Adalbert   S. 105
Begas-von Parmentier, Luise   S. 105
Bendler, Johann Christoph   S. 17
Bernauer, Rudolf   S. 72
Bernhard, Lucian   S. 76–77
Bernstein, Felicie und Carl   S. 84–85
Blumenthal, Leonhard von   S. 82
Bode, Wilhelm von   S. 22, 36, 40, 46, 48, 62, 74, 84, 86, 90, 92, 94, 96, 106
Botticelli, Sandro   S. 22, 46
Breslauer, Alfred   S. 95
Brütt, Adolf   S. 82
Bühling, Carl Wilhelm   S. 33
Busse, Carl   S. 99, 101
Cassirer, Bruno   S. 10, 50
Cassirer, Paul   S. 10, 32–33, 50–51, 96, 100
Chagall, Marc   S. 64–65
Curtius, Clara   S. 24
Curtius, Ernst   S. 10, 24, 84
Degas, Edgar   S. 96
Dernburg, Hermann   S. 68
Dirksen, Willibald von   S. 36–37
Dohm, Ernst   S. 26–27, 74
Dohm, Hedwig   S. 26–27
Durieux, Tilla   S. 32–33, 72

Dybwad, Peter   S. 41
Dyck, Anthonis van   S. 92
Elias, Julius   S. 10, 24
Emmerich, Jürgen und Paul   S. 15
Flechtheim, Alfred   S. 108–109
Friedländer, Max Jacob   S. 106–107
Friedmann, Ernst   S. 68–69
Friedrich III., Kaiser   S. 12, 82, 82
Friedrich Wilhelm IV., preußischer König   S. 17
Gilly, Friedrich   S. 17–18
Gogh, Vincent van   S. 96, 108
Graupe, Paul   S. 87–89, 98
Gropius, Martin   S. 17–18
Gutbrod, Rolf   S. 5, 19–20
Hals, Frans   S. 22, 92
Heidecke, Christian   S. 87, 91
Helmholtz, Hermann von   S. 82
Herrmann, Curt   S. 84
Hilmer und Sattler (Heinz Hilmer und Christoph Sattler)   S. 5, 20
Hirschwald, Hermann   S. 69
Hitzig, Georg   S. 16–18, 42–43, 49
Hoffacker, Karl   S. 73
Hoffmann, Ludwig und Marie   S. 38–39, 41
Hollein, Hans   S. 6
Hude, Hermann von der und Julius Hennicke   S. 75
Huldschinsky, Oscar   S. 22–23
Huldschinsky, Paul   S. 89, 98–99
Ihne, Ernst Eberhard von   S. 48–49, 74
Kandinsky, Wassily   S. 64

Kappel, Marcus   S. 92–93
Karajan, Herbert von   S. 12
Kayser, Heinrich und Karl von Großheim (Büro)   S. 31, 97
Keller und Reiner, Kunstsalon   S. 60–61, 69
Kemper, Johann Wilhelm   S. 16
Kessler, Harry Graf von   S. 34, 57, 66–67, 74
Klee, Paul   S. 64
Klingenberg, Ernst   S. 59, 105
Klinger, Max   S. 84
Kolbe, Georg   S. 10, 34, 100–101
Kopetzky, Wilhelm   S. 30
Krüger, Hans Carl   S. 62
Langhans, Carl Gotthard   S. 17–18
Leistikow, Walter   S. 84
Lenné, Peter Joseph   S. 9, 13, 16
Lepke, Rudolph   S. 62–63
Lepsius, Reinhold   S. 84
Lessing, Julius   S. 57, 86
Lewinsky, Karl   S. 60
Liebermann, Felix   S. 103
Liebermann, Georg   S. 87
Liebermann, Max   S. 24, 44, 84
Lipperheide, Franz und Frieda von   S. 34, 56–57
Lippmann, Friedrich   S. 85–86
Löbich & Sohn   S. 25
Macke, August   S. 64
Manet, Édouard   S. 85, 96
Mantegna, Andrea   S. 94
Meier-Graefe, Julius   S. 104

Meinhard, Carl   S. 72
Menzel, Adolph von   S. 10, 28–29, 74, 84, 92
Messel, Alfred   S. 17–18, 38, 47
Meyerbeer, Giacomo   S. 74–75
Mies van der Rohe, Ludwig   S. 5, 20
Münter, Gabriele   S. 64
Olfers, Marie von   S. 10, 34–35
Oppenheim, Benoit   S. 90–91
Parey, Paul   S. 30–31
Persius, Ludwig   S. 18
Picasso, Pablo   S. 108
Piombo, Sebastiano del   S. 22
Pissarro, Camille   S. 85, 96
Preußen, Augusta von   S. 17
Preußen, Margarete von   S. 13
Preußen, Sigismund von   S. 12
Preußen, Victoria von   S. 13
Raffael da Urbino   S. 22
Rathenau, Emil   S. 44–45, 103
Rathenau, Walther   S. 44–45
Rehnig, Otto   S. 79
Rembrandt Harmenszoon van Rijn   S. 22, 92, 94
Renoir, Auguste   S. 96
Richter, Cornelie   S. 10, 74–75
Rilke, Rainer Maria   S. 34
Rubens, Peter Paul   S. 22, 92
Scharoun, Hans   S. 5, 6, 13, 18–20
Schinkel, Karl Friedrich   S. 17–18
Schmitz, Bruno   S. 61
Schüttler, Carl Ludwig   S. 51

Schultz, Johann Ludwig   S. 51
Schwatlo, Carl   S. 95
Schweitzer, Heinrich   S. 111
Simon, Eduard   S. 46–47
Simon, James   S. 46, 94–95
Sisley, Alfred   S. 85, 96
Speyer, Leonora   S. 109
Strauch, A. W.   S. 93
Stieber, Wilhelm   S. 25
Streichenberg, August Julius   S. 35
Stüler, Friedrich August   S. 5, 15, 17–18
Reinhardt, Max   S. 74
Tiepolo, Giovanni Battista   S. 22, 47–48
Tschudi, Hugo von   S. 74, 84
Velde, Henry van de   S. 51, 67, 69, 74
Walden, Herwarth und Nell   S. 64–65
Weber, Hermann   S. 69–70
Weisbach, Valentin S. 37–38, 40–41, 86–87
Weisbach, Werner   S. 40–41, 84
Werner, Anton von   S. 10, 58–59
Wilhelm I., Kaiser   S. 17
Wilhelm II., Kaiser   S. 16, 77, 83
Wisniewski, Edgar   S. 19
Wolffenberg, Adolf und Gustav   S. 62
Wollenberg, Adolf   S. 63
Zuckmayer, Carl   S. 10

Für die Staatlichen Museen zu Berlin herausgegeben von Michael Eissenhauer
www.smb.museum

© 2019 Michael Imhof Verlag, Petersberg und
Staatliche Museen zu Berlin – Preußischer Kulturbesitz

Publikationskoordination für die Museen: Andrea Schindelmeier, Anna Wegenschimmel
Übersetzung ins Englische: allround Fremdsprachen GmbH, Ü-Werk GmbH

Druck: optimal media GmbH, Röbel/Müritz

Printed in the EU
Alle Rechte vorbehalten
ISBN 978-3-7319-0789-3